10 Powerful Productivity Hacks to Boost Your Income

By

Oscar T. Johnson

Copyright © 2024 by Oscar T. Johnson.
All rights reserved.

No part of this publication may be reproduced, distributed, or transmitted in any form or by any means, including photocopying, recording, or other electronic or mechanical methods, without the prior written permission of the publisher, except in the case of brief quotations embodied in critical reviews and certain other noncommercial uses permitted by copyright law.

Table Of Content

Introduction... 5
    Why Time Management is Crucial for Earning More..5
    Unveiling the Secrets of Increased Productivity and Revenue... 10

Master Your Time Management................. 15
    The Power of Prioritization...............................15
    The Art of Time Blocking................................ 24

Conquer the To-Do List............................ 34
    The Two-Minute Rule..................................... 34
    The Pomodoro Technique...............................43

Harness the Power of Automation............ 53
    Utilize Technology to Streamline Repetitive Tasks.. 53
    Leverage Templates and Presets......................63

Tame Your Inbox and Manage Communication.. 73
    Unsubscribe from Unnecessary Emails and Newsletters.. 73
    Batch Processing Emails................................ 83

Learn to Say No (Without Feeling Guilty)..92
    Identify Projects and Requests That Drain Your Time and Resources.. 92
    Offer Alternative Solutions or Referrals When Appropriate... 100

Embrace the Power of Outsourcing......... 109
    Delegate Tasks That Others Can Do More Efficiently..109
    Consider Virtual Assistants, Freelancers, or Online Tools... 117

Create a Dedicated Workspace (and Keep it Organized)... **128**
    Designate a Specific Area for Focused Work. 128
    Maintain a Clutter-Free Environment with Organizational Systems................................ 138

Cultivate Healthy Habits for Peak Performance... **149**
    Prioritize Quality Sleep for Improved Focus and Energy... 149
    Eat Nutritious Foods and Stay Hydrated....... 159

Eliminate Distractions and Stay Focused.170
    Silence Notifications and Put Your Phone Away. 170
    Identify and Eliminate Time-Sinks................ 180

Track Your Progress and Celebrate Milestones... **193**
    Apps and Journals for Tracking Progress...... 193
    Reward Yourself for Reaching Milestones.... 206

Conclusion.. **219**
    Recap of the 10 Powerful Productivity Hacks 219
    The Road to Earning More with Increased Efficiency and Time Management................. 222
    Embracing Continuous Improvement and Refining Your Strategies............................... 226

Additional Info.. **231**
    Tools, Apps, and Resources to Enhance Productivity..231
    Creating a Personalized Productivity System that Works for You... 235
    Additional Strategies for Specific Industries or Work Styles... 240

Introduction

Why Time Management is Crucial for Earning More

Why Time Management is Crucial for Earning More: Mastering Your Minutes to Maximize Your Income

In today's competitive world, time is a valuable asset. It's the currency with which we trade for income, career advancement, and overall well-being. Yet, many of us struggle to manage this precious resource effectively. Here's why time management is crucial for earning more and how mastering your minutes can unlock greater financial potential:

1. Unleashing Peak Performance: Effective time management allows you to prioritize tasks strategically, focusing your energy on high-value activities that directly contribute to revenue generation. By eliminating time-wasters and streamlining your workflow, you get more done in less time. This translates to completing projects faster, taking on additional work opportunities, and ultimately, boosting your earning potential. Imagine the financial rewards of consistently delivering high-quality work within compressed timelines – time management is the key to unlocking this efficiency.

2. Conquering Procrastination's Price Tag: Procrastination is a productivity killer that silently eats away at your earning potential. When tasks pile up, it becomes overwhelming, leading to missed deadlines, frustrated clients, and potentially, lost business opportunities. Time management equips you with tools and techniques to tackle tasks head-on, preventing procrastination and ensuring you capitalize on income-generating possibilities. By staying ahead of the curve and meeting deadlines consistently, you build trust with clients and position yourself for repeat business and referrals – a significant advantage in today's competitive landscape.

3. Sharpening Your Focus, Sharpening Your Results: Feeling overwhelmed by a never-ending to-do list can lead to scattered thinking and decreased focus. This can manifest in errors, missed details, and ultimately, work that falls short of expectations. Effective time management techniques like creating schedules, prioritizing tasks, and utilizing time-blocking strategies help declutter your mind, allowing you to focus on the work at hand and deliver high-quality results. This translates to increased client satisfaction, improved reputation, and potentially, higher earning potential. Imagine the financial rewards of consistently exceeding client expectations – time management is the key to achieving this focus and precision.

4. Building Trustworthy Client Relationships: Meeting deadlines and exceeding client expectations are crucial for building trust and securing repeat business. Time management helps you schedule client meetings effectively, manage project timelines efficiently, and deliver high-quality work on time. This reliability fosters positive client relationships, leading to long-term partnerships and potentially, increased income streams. Reliable service builds trust, and trust translates to repeat business and referrals – a powerful formula for boosting your earning potential.

5. Investing in Your Future Earning Power: When your schedule is constantly overflowing, it becomes difficult to dedicate time to learning and skill development. Effective time management frees up valuable minutes for you to invest in acquiring new skills or refining existing ones. This can make you a more valuable asset in the job market, potentially leading to promotions, higher paying opportunities, and a long-term boost in your earning potential. Imagine the financial rewards of constantly expanding your skillset and expertise – time management is the key to creating the space for this investment in your future.

6. From Overwhelmed to Empowered: Chronic stress associated with feeling overwhelmed and overworked can negatively impact your health, well-being, and ultimately, your productivity. Time management helps you stay organized and in control, reducing stress levels and promoting a sense of accomplishment. This improved well-being can translate to increased energy, motivation, and ultimately, a more productive and financially rewarding work life. By managing your time effectively, you can avoid burnout and create a sustainable work style that allows you to maintain your earning potential for years to come.

7. Beyond the Urgent, Towards the Strategic: When your days are consumed with managing the immediate, it's easy to lose sight of your long-term goals. Effective time management creates space for strategic thinking. You can dedicate time to analyze your career path, identify income-generating opportunities, set realistic and achievable goals, and develop a roadmap for achieving them. This strategic approach keeps you focused on the bigger picture and ensures your daily efforts are aligned with your financial aspirations.

8. Fostering a Proactive Work Ethic: Time management encourages a proactive approach to work. Instead of reacting to urgent demands and scrambling to meet deadlines, you can anticipate tasks and plan your day strategically. This proactive approach allows you to identify potential challenges and find solutions before they escalate, preventing setbacks and ensuring smooth workflow, ultimately leading to more consistent income and a reputation for reliability.

9. Creating Work-Life Balance for Sustainable Success: A healthy work-life balance is crucial for long-term productivity and career success. Effective time management helps you manage your workload efficiently, ensuring you dedicate enough time to both work and personal life. This prevents burnout and promotes a sustainable work style, allowing you to maintain your earning potential for years to come.

10. Empowers You to Take Control:
Time management is about taking control of your day and your career. It empowers you to make conscious choices about how you spend your time, ensuring your efforts are aligned with your financial goals. This sense of control fosters confidence and motivation, leading to a more fulfilling and financially rewarding work experience.

In conclusion, time management is not just about getting things done; it's about strategically investing your time to maximize your earning potential. By mastering your minutes, you can unlock greater efficiency, reduce stress, and create a sustainable path to financial success.

Unveiling the Secrets of Increased Productivity and Revenue

Unveiling the Secrets of Increased Productivity and Revenue: Unlock Your Earning Potential

In today's fast-paced world, maximizing your income requires more than just hard work. It demands **strategic time management, efficient workflows, and a focus on high-value activities**. This guide delves into the secrets of increased productivity and revenue, revealing strategies to transform your work style and unlock your true earning potential.

The Power of Time Management:

Time is your most valuable asset. It's the currency with which you trade for income. Mastering your time allows you to:

- **Prioritize Tasks Strategically:** Focus energy on high-value activities that directly impact your income. By eliminating time-wasters and streamlining your workflow, you get more done in less time, leading to faster project completion and the ability to take on more opportunities.

- **Conquer Procrastination's Price Tag:** Procrastination is a productivity killer that steals potential earnings. Time management equips you with tools and techniques to tackle tasks head-on, ensuring you capitalize on income-generating possibilities.

- **Sharpen Your Focus, Sharpen Your Results:** When overwhelmed by to-do lists, focus scatters and results suffer. Time management strategies like scheduling, prioritization, and time-blocking help declutter your mind, allowing you to deliver high-quality work that exceeds client expectations, building trust and potentially leading to higher earning potential.

Building a Productivity Powerhouse:

Beyond time management, cultivate habits for peak performance:

- **Craft a Dedicated Workspace:** Designate a specific area for focused work, minimizing distractions and promoting a productive mindset.

- **Embrace Automation:** Utilize technology to streamline repetitive tasks. Email autoresponders, scheduling tools, and project management software free up valuable time for more high-value activities.

- **Harness the Power of Outsourcing:** Delegate tasks that others can do more efficiently. Virtual assistants, freelancers, and online tools can expand your skillset and free up precious time.

Prioritization for Profit:

Not all tasks are created equal. Mastering prioritization allows you to:

- **Identify High-Impact Activities:** Distinguish between urgent tasks and those that significantly contribute to your income goals. Focus on the latter first.

- **The Eisenhower Matrix:** This framework categorizes tasks based on urgency and importance, helping you prioritize, delegate, or eliminate activities.

Taming the To-Do List:

Effective to-do list management ensures you stay on track:

- **The Two-Minute Rule:** Tackle small tasks immediately, streamlining your workflow and reducing procrastination.

- **The Pomodoro Technique:** Work in focused sprints – short work intervals followed by breaks – to maximize concentration and combat fatigue.

Eliminating Distractions and Staying Focused:

Minimize distractions for optimal productivity:

- **Silence Notifications:** Turn off phone notifications and silence email alerts, regaining control of your time and minimizing interruptions.

- **Identify and Eliminate Time-Sinks:** Recognize and curb activities like social media browsing that drain your focus. Utilize apps or settings to block these distractions.

Healthy Habits for Peak Performance:

Your well-being directly impacts your productivity:

- **Prioritize Quality Sleep:** Aim for consistent sleep to improve focus, energy, and overall well-being.

- **Fuel Your Focus:** Eat nutritious foods and stay hydrated for sustained energy. A healthy diet promotes physical and mental well-being, preventing crashes and maintaining focus.

Continuous Improvement and Long-Term Success:

- **Track Your Progress:** Use time management apps or bullet journals to monitor your progress, identify areas for improvement, and maintain motivation.

- **Celebrate Milestones:** Reward yourself for reaching milestones and completing tasks. This reinforces positive behavior and keeps you motivated.

- **Embrace Continuous Learning:** Investing in your skillset opens doors to higher-paying opportunities. Dedicate time to learning new skills and refining existing ones.

By implementing these strategies, you'll unlock a new level of productivity. You'll have more control over your time, achieve exceptional results, and ultimately, **maximize your earning potential**. Remember, building a successful career is a journey, not a destination. Embrace continuous learning, refine your strategies, and watch your income soar!

Master Your Time Management

The Power of Prioritization

Identifying Urgent and Important Tasks: Mastering Your To-Do List

Feeling overwhelmed by a never-ending to-do list? Struggling to distinguish between tasks that demand immediate attention and those that contribute to your long-term goals? You're not alone. In today's fast-paced world, mastering the art of identifying urgent and important tasks is crucial for maximizing productivity and achieving success. This guide equips you with effective strategies to categorize your workload, prioritize strategically, and conquer your to-do list with confidence.

Understanding the Difference:

The key to effective prioritization lies in understanding the fundamental difference between urgent and important tasks:

- **Urgent Tasks:** These tasks demand immediate attention and can have significant consequences if neglected. They are typically time-sensitive and often involve external pressures. Examples include meeting deadlines, responding to critical client emails, or addressing technical emergencies.

- **Important Tasks:** These tasks contribute significantly to your long-term goals and overall well-being. They are not necessarily time-sensitive but hold strategic value for your future success. Examples include developing new skills, building relationships with potential clients, proactive project planning, or maintaining healthy habits.

Identifying Urgent Tasks:

Urgent tasks typically manifest themselves through clear deadlines, external pressure, and potential for immediate negative consequences if neglected. Here are some indicators that a task is urgent:

- **Has a fixed deadline:** Deadlines create a sense of urgency, particularly when they are approaching soon. Tasks with immediate deadlines, like presentations or reports due the next day, fall into this category.

- **Involves potential consequences:** Certain tasks, if left unaddressed, can have negative repercussions. Responding to a client complaint or fixing a technical issue that impacts operations are examples of urgent tasks with potential consequences.

- **External pressure exists:** Deadlines imposed by others, urgent requests from clients or colleagues, or unexpected events can create external pressure, making a task urgent. Responding to a critical email from a supervisor or dealing with a sudden server outage would be considered urgent due to external pressure.

Identifying Important Tasks:

Important tasks may not have immediate deadlines but contribute significantly to your long-term success and well-being. Here are some ways to identify important tasks:

- **Alignment with long-term goals:** Evaluate if the task contributes to your overall goals. This could include skill development, career advancement, personal growth, or maintaining work-life balance. Taking a course relevant to your field or attending a networking event would be considered important due to their alignment with long-term career goals.

- **Prevents future problems:** Certain tasks, while not urgent, are important to prevent future issues. Examples include preventive maintenance for equipment, creating a backup system for your computer data, or attending a regular health check-up.

- **Improves efficiency or performance:** Tasks that streamline your workflow, enhance your skills, or improve overall efficiency fall under the important category. Automating repetitive tasks, learning a new productivity tool, or attending a relevant professional development seminar are examples of important tasks that enhance your performance.

Prioritizing Effectively:

Once you can distinguish between urgent and important tasks, effective prioritization becomes possible. A common prioritization framework is the Eisenhower Matrix, which categorizes tasks based on urgency and importance. Here's how to apply it:

- **List all your tasks:** Create a comprehensive inventory of everything on your plate, both personal and professional.

- **Analyze each task:** Evaluate each task based on its urgency and importance, placing it in the appropriate quadrant of the Eisenhower Matrix (Do First, Schedule, Delegate, Eliminate).

- **Take action:** Focus on completing tasks in the "Do First" quadrant first. Schedule time for tasks in the "Schedule" quadrant. Delegate or outsource tasks in the "Delegate" quadrant. Eliminate activities in the "Eliminate" quadrant.

Mastering Your Workflow:

By mastering the art of identifying urgent and important tasks, you can conquer your to-do list and transform your workflow:

- **Focus on high-impact tasks:** Prioritize tasks in the "Do First" and "Schedule" quadrants of the Eisenhower Matrix. These tasks contribute directly to your goals and deadlines.

- **Reduce stress and overwhelm:** By categorizing your tasks, you gain clarity on your workload, reducing stress and anxiety associated with a never-ending to-do list.

- **Improve time management:** Prioritization allows you to allocate time strategically, ensuring you meet deadlines and deliver high-quality results for urgent tasks while dedicating time for important, long-term goals.

- **Boost productivity and efficiency:** Focusing on the right tasks frees up valuable time and energy, allowing you to achieve more in less time. Eliminating distractions and time-wasters further optimizes your productivity.

Mastering your to-do list requires effective task identification and prioritization. By distinguishing between urgency and importance, you can focus on activities that truly matter, achieve your goals more efficiently, and maximize your productivity. Remember, the Eisenhower Matrix is a powerful tool to organize and prioritize tasks based on urgency and importance. Implement it to gain clarity and control over your workload.

Delegating, Scheduling, and Eliminating Activities: Streamlining Your Workflow for Peak Performance

Feeling overwhelmed by your to-do list? Drowning in a sea of tasks and struggling to find the time to achieve your goals? The key to success lies in mastering the art of **delegation, scheduling, and elimination.** This guide unlocks powerful strategies to streamline your workflow, free up valuable time, and empower you to focus on what truly matters.

Delegation: Empowering Others for Shared Success

Delegation is not about dumping tasks on others. It's about strategically assigning activities to maximize efficiency and leverage the expertise of others. Here's how to delegate effectively:

- **Identify Tasks for Delegation:** Not all tasks require your direct attention. Consider delegating routine or repetitive activities, low-skill tasks, or anything someone else can learn to do effectively. Examples include data entry, scheduling appointments, or social media management.

- **Choose the Right Person:** Match the task to the skillset and experience of the individual. Consider who on your team possesses the necessary skills and capacity to handle the delegated task efficiently.

- **Clear Communication is Key:** Provide clear instructions, outlining the task's purpose, desired workflow, and expected outcomes. Offer necessary resources and training to ensure successful completion.

- **Set Deadlines and Expectations:** Establish clear deadlines for the delegated tasks and set realistic expectations for quality and deliverables. Encourage open communication to address any questions or concerns.

- **Empower and Provide Feedback:** Offer trust and autonomy when you delegate. While providing support, avoid micromanaging. Offer constructive feedback to ensure continued improvement in future delegations.

Scheduling: Creating Time for What Matters Most

Scheduling is not just about keeping track of appointments. It's about carving out dedicated time in your day for specific tasks, ensuring important activities receive the focus they deserve. Here's how to create an effective schedule:

- **Identify Key Time Blocks:** Allocate time blocks for your most crucial tasks, such as completing urgent projects, brainstorming new ideas, or conducting strategic planning. These are your "Do First" activities as defined by the Eisenhower Matrix.

- **Consider Your Energy Levels:** Schedule demanding tasks during your peak productivity hours. Assign less demanding tasks to times when your energy dips. Understanding your personal rhythm allows for optimal utilization of your time.

- **Buffer Time for the Unexpected:** Allocate buffer time within your schedule to account for unforeseen circumstances, interruptions, or delays. This prevents a domino effect on the rest of your day.

- **Utilize Scheduling Tools:** Harness the power of digital calendars, task management apps, or project management software. These tools help you visualize your schedule, track tasks, and set reminders for deadlines.

- **Review and Adapt:** Schedules are not set in stone. Revisit your schedule regularly and adapt it to your project progress, priorities, and unforeseen changes. Flexibility is essential for maintaining an efficient and productive workflow.

Elimination: Less is More for Maximum Focus

While delegating frees up time, elimination focuses on removing unnecessary activities altogether. Be ruthless in identifying and eliminating activities that drain your time and offer little to no value. Here's how to eliminate effectively:

- **Identify Time-Wasters:** Be honest with yourself. Analyze your daily routine and identify activities that consume time without delivering results. Examples include excessive social media browsing, multitasking, or attending irrelevant meetings.

- **Apply the Pareto Principle (80/20 Rule):** This principle suggests 80% of your results come from 20% of your efforts. Identify the activities that generate minimal value (20%) and eliminate them, allowing you to focus on the high-impact activities (20%) that deliver 80% of your results.

- **Learn to Say No:** Don't be afraid to politely decline tasks or requests that don't align with your priorities or goals. Offering alternative solutions or delegating when appropriate can be helpful strategies.

- **Minimize Distractions:** Turn off unnecessary notifications, silence your phone during focused work sessions, and consider utilizing time-blocking apps to create a distraction-free environment.

- **Automate When Possible:** Identify repetitive tasks that technology can handle. Utilize email autoresponders, project management software, or online tools to automate routine processes, freeing up your time for more strategic endeavors.

Delegation, scheduling, and elimination are powerful tools for transforming your workflow and maximizing your productivity. By leveraging these strategies, you can free up valuable time, achieve optimal focus, and ultimately, achieve your goals with greater efficiency and success. Remember, less is often more. Focus on strategically delegating, scheduling, and eliminating activities to make room for what truly

The Art of Time Blocking

Creating Dedicated Blocks for Focused Work: Unleash Your Inner Powerhouse

In today's digital age, distractions abound. Between overflowing inboxes, constant notifications, and the allure of social media, maintaining focused work can feel like an uphill battle. The key to unlocking peak productivity lies in **creating dedicated blocks for focused work**. These uninterrupted time periods allow you to delve deep into important tasks, achieve optimal results, and ultimately, conquer the chaos of a busy world.

The Power of Focused Work:

- **Enhanced Productivity:** Focused work allows you to enter a state of "flow," where distractions fade away and your attention is fully engaged. This significantly increases productivity, enabling you to accomplish more in less time.

- **Improved Quality of Work:** When distractions are minimized, your cognitive function is optimized. This leads to a higher quality of work, with fewer errors and a greater level of detail and accuracy.

- **Reduced Stress and Anxiety:** The constant context-switching caused by distractions can be mentally draining. Focused work sessions provide a much-needed respite, reducing stress and anxiety associated with feeling overwhelmed.

- **Enhanced Creativity and Problem-Solving:** Without distractions, your mind has the space to explore ideas, make connections, and solve problems more effectively. Focused work fosters an environment conducive to creative thinking and innovation.

Crafting Your Ideal Focus Block:

Here's how to design dedicated blocks for focused work that enhance your productivity and well-being:

- **Identify Your Peak Performance Hours:** We all have times when our energy levels and focus are naturally higher. Schedule your focused work blocks during these peak performance hours, maximizing your mental stamina and cognitive function.

- **Choose the Right Duration:** The ideal length of a focus block varies depending on the activity and your personal preferences. Experiment with different durations, starting with shorter blocks (25-minute increments) and gradually increasing the length as you build focus stamina. The Pomodoro Technique, which utilizes 25-minute work intervals followed by short breaks, can be a powerful tool for managing focus blocks.

- **Communicate Your Focus Time:** Inform colleagues and clients about your dedicated focus blocks to minimize interruptions. Utilize tools like "Do Not Disturb" settings or calendar blocks to communicate your unavailability.

- **Eliminate Distractions:** Turn off notifications on your phone and computer, silence your workspace, and close unnecessary browser tabs.

Consider utilizing noise-cancelling headphones to further minimize external distractions.

- **Prepare Your Workspace:** Declutter your work area to create a visually calming environment conducive to focused work. Ensure good lighting, comfortable seating, and access to necessary materials.

- **Utilize Focus Tools:** Explore apps and tools designed to promote focused work. Some options include website blockers, time trackers, and noise cancellation apps. Experiment to find tools that complement your work style and preference.

- **Plan Your Work in Advance:** Before diving into your focus block, have a clear roadmap of the task at hand. List specific goals you want to achieve within the block, identify any necessary resources, and outline a plan for tackling the task efficiently.

- **Schedule Breaks:** Focus doesn't mean working non-stop. Schedule short breaks (5-10 minutes) between your focus blocks to allow your mind to rest and recharge. Get up and move around, stretch, or step outside for some fresh air.

- **Review and Adapt:** As you implement dedicated focus blocks, analyze their effectiveness. Adjust the length, timing, or strategies based on your experience. The key is to find what works best for you and allows you to maintain sustained focus.

Beyond the Block: Maintaining Focus Throughout the Day

In addition to creating dedicated focus blocks, cultivate habits that support focused work throughout the day:

- **Prioritize ruthlessly:** Identify the most important tasks and allocate dedicated focus blocks for them. Eliminate or delegate less crucial activities to maximize the impact of your focused work periods.

- **Minimize multitasking:** Focus on completing one task at a time. Multitasking divides attention and ultimately hinders productivity.

- **Maintain a healthy routine:** Ensure adequate sleep, eat nutritious meals, and stay hydrated. These lifestyle habits contribute significantly to your ability to focus and maintain mental clarity.

Creating dedicated blocks for focused work is a game-changer for maximizing your productivity and achieving your goals. By implementing these strategies and tailoring them to your individual needs, you can conquer distractions, unleash your full potential, and thrive in a world that constantly demands your attention. Remember, focused work is an investment in your success – carve out the time and watch your results soar.

Taming the Tigers of Distraction: Maximizing Output in a Distracted World

The modern workplace is a battleground for attention. Between overflowing inboxes, social media notifications, and the allure of multitasking, staying focused and productive can feel like an Olympic feat. However, fear not! By implementing strategies to **minimize distractions and maximize output**, you can reclaim control of your workday and achieve remarkable results.

The High Cost of Distraction:

- **Reduced Productivity:** Distractions derail your train of thought, forcing you to constantly refocus. This significantly impacts the amount of work you can complete in a given timeframe.

- **Increased Errors:** When your attention is divided, the likelihood of errors increases. This can lead to rework, missed deadlines, and ultimately, frustration and inefficiency.

- **Decreased Creativity:** Distractions stifle the flow of ideas and hinder creative thinking. Focused work is essential for generating innovative solutions and tackling problems effectively.

- **Mental Fatigue:** The constant context-switching caused by distractions can be mentally draining. This leads to fatigue, decreased motivation, and ultimately, reduced output.

Building a Fortress of Focus:

Here's your arsenal of strategies to combat distractions and maximize your output:

- **Identify Your Kryptonite:** Recognize your biggest distractors. Is it social media, email notifications, or the lure of a colleague's conversation? Once you know your weaknesses, you can develop strategies to address them.

- **Embrace Time Management Techniques:** Utilize time management tools like the Eisenhower Matrix to prioritize tasks and schedule dedicated focus blocks for high-impact activities. The Pomodoro Technique, with its 25-minute work intervals followed by short breaks, can be a powerful tool for managing distractions within your focus blocks.

- **Craft a Distraction-Free Zone:** Designate a workspace that minimizes distractions. Declutter your desk, silence your phone, and consider utilizing noise-canceling headphones to block out external noise.

- **Harness the Power of Technology:** Technology can be a double-edged sword. Utilize apps and browser extensions that block distracting websites and social media. Explore tools like time trackers or focus timers to maintain awareness of your workflow.

- **Communicate Your Needs:** Inform colleagues and clients about your focus time. Utilize "Do Not Disturb" settings on communication platforms or clearly communicate your unavailability during dedicated work blocks.

- **Practice Mindfulness:** Mindfulness techniques like meditation can help you develop greater focus and awareness. Taking a few minutes to center yourself before a focused work block can significantly improve your ability to resist distractions.

- **Embrace Single-Tasking:** Multitasking is a myth. Focus on completing one task at a time to achieve higher quality results and maximize efficiency.

- **Schedule Breaks:** While focus is key, taking short breaks is essential. Step away from your desk, stretch, or grab a healthy snack to recharge your mind and prevent burnout.

- **Reward Yourself:** Positive reinforcement goes a long way. Celebrate your accomplishments at the end of a productive focus block. This motivates you to maintain focus and achieve even greater results in the future.

Beyond the Tactics: Cultivating Focus-Friendly Habits

In addition to these strategies, consider these habits to promote sustained focus throughout your day:

- **Prioritize Sleep:** Aim for 7-8 hours of quality sleep each night. Adequate sleep is crucial for maintaining cognitive function and focus.

- **Eat Nutritiously:** Fuel your brain with nutritious foods that provide sustained energy. Avoid sugary snacks and processed foods that can lead to energy crashes and decreased focus.

- **Stay Hydrated:** Dehydration can significantly impact cognitive function. Drink plenty of water throughout the day to maintain focus and mental clarity.

- **Exercise Regularly:** Physical activity improves circulation and mental well-being, both of which contribute to increased focus and productivity.

- **Minimize Stress:** Chronic stress can hinder your ability to focus. Develop healthy stress management techniques like meditation, exercise, or spending time in nature.

Minimizing distractions and maximizing output is a continuous journey. By implementing these strategies and tailoring them to your individual needs, you can create a work environment conducive to focus and achievement. Remember, conquering distractions is an investment in your success. With dedication and the right tools, you can reclaim control of your workday and unlock your full potential.

Conquer the To-Do List

The Two-Minute Rule

Conquering Chaos: Streamlining Your Workflow and Reducing Procrastination

Do you ever feel like there just aren't enough hours in the day? Are your to-do lists a constant source of stress, and procrastination your worst enemy? You're not alone. In today's fast-paced world, streamlining your workflow and overcoming procrastination are essential skills for achieving success. This guide equips you with powerful strategies to transform your work style, boost productivity, and finally conquer that ever-growing to-do list.

The Pitfalls of a Chaotic Workflow:

- **Reduced Productivity:** A cluttered and disorganized workflow leads to wasted time searching for information, switching between tasks, and inefficiently completing projects.

- **Increased Stress and Anxiety:** The feeling of being overwhelmed by a disorganized workload can lead to significant stress and anxiety, hindering your ability to focus and perform at your best.

- **Missed Deadlines and Lower Quality Work:** A chaotic workflow makes it difficult to meet deadlines and can lead to rushed and error-prone work.

Streamlining for Success:

Here's how to create a streamlined workflow that empowers you to achieve more with less:

- **Embrace Automation:** Utilize technology to automate repetitive tasks. Explore email autoresponders, project management software, or online tools to streamline data entry, scheduling, or basic design tasks.

- **Prioritize Ruthlessly:** Not all tasks are created equal. Utilize the Eisenhower Matrix to categorize tasks based on urgency and importance. Focus on completing high-impact tasks first and delegate, eliminate, or schedule less crucial activities.

- **Batch Similar Tasks:** Group similar tasks together to minimize context switching. For example, dedicate specific times to respond to emails, return phone calls, or review reports.

- **Create a Defined Workspace:** Designate a specific area for focused work. Organize your workspace logically to minimize distractions and promote efficiency. Invest in ergonomic furniture to prevent fatigue.

- **Utilize Time Management Techniques:** Techniques like the Pomodoro Technique (25 minutes of work followed by a short break) can help you maintain focus and manage time effectively.

- **Maintain Clear Communication:** Keep colleagues and clients informed about project progress and deadlines. This reduces the need for back-and-forth communication and streamlines workflow.

Procrastination: The Productivity Killer

Procrastination is the thief of time, robbing you of precious productivity and creating unnecessary stress. Here's how to overcome it:

- **Identify Your Triggers:** Recognize the situations or emotions that trigger your procrastination. Are you overwhelmed by a complex task, or do you find yourself checking social media for a quick "break" that spirals out of control?

- **Break Down Large Tasks:** Large, daunting tasks can be overwhelming, leading to procrastination. Break down complex projects into smaller, more manageable steps. This creates a clear roadmap and makes the task seem less intimidating.

- **Set SMART Goals:** Set Specific, Measurable, Achievable, Relevant, and Time-bound goals. These SMART goals provide clarity and direction, motivating you to take action and avoid procrastination.

- **Reward Yourself:** Positive reinforcement is a powerful tool. Acknowledge and reward yourself for completing tasks on time. This reinforces positive behavior and encourages you to stay on track.

- **Embrace the Power of "Just Start":** Often, the hardest part is simply beginning. Commit to starting a task for just a few minutes. Momentum often builds, and you'll find yourself completing more than you initially planned.

- **Eliminate Distractions:** Silence notifications, turn off social media, and create a distraction-free environment to minimize procrastination triggers and allow you to focus on the task at hand.

Building a Sustainable System for Success

Streamlining your workflow and overcoming procrastination are continuous processes. Here are some additional tips to cultivate a sustainable system for success:

- **Maintain a Healthy Routine:** Prioritize quality sleep, regular exercise, and a balanced diet. These lifestyle habits fuel your energy levels, improve focus, and enhance your ability to manage your workload effectively.

- **Minimize Multitasking:** Focus on completing one task at a time. Multitasking is a myth that leads to errors and decreased efficiency.

- **Schedule Breaks:** While focus is crucial, planned breaks are essential to prevent burnout. Step away from your desk, stretch, or take a walk to recharge your mind and return to your work with renewed focus.

- **Learn to Say No:** Don't be afraid to politely decline additional tasks or requests that don't align with your priorities or capacity.

Celebrate Your Achievements: Take time to acknowledge your progress and celebrate your accomplishments. This boosts motivation and reinforces positive work habits.

Streamlining your workflow and overcoming procrastination are two sides of the same coin. By implementing these strategies, you can create an efficient work environment, conquer distractions, and finally achieve your full potential. Remember, consistency is key. The more you prioritize ruthlessly, streamline your processes, and actively address procrastination, the easier it will become to maintain a productive and fulfilling work style.

Decluttering Your Mind: Freeing Up Mental Space for More Important Tasks

Do you ever feel like your brain is a cluttered attic, overflowing with unfinished tasks, nagging worries, and a constant stream of information? This mental clutter can be a significant drain on your focus, creativity, and overall well-being. The good news is, you can reclaim control and free up mental space for what truly matters. This guide equips you with powerful strategies to declutter your mind, enhance your focus, and unlock your full potential.

The Burden of Mental Clutter:

- **Reduced Cognitive Function:** Mental clutter consumes valuable cognitive resources, making it difficult to focus on tasks at hand, hindering your ability to learn, problem-solve, and make sound decisions.

- **Increased Stress and Anxiety:** The constant hum of mental noise can lead to chronic stress and anxiety, impacting your emotional well-being and overall health.

- **Diminished Creativity:** A cluttered mind struggles to generate new ideas and think creatively. Freeing up mental space allows for increased creativity and innovation.

- **Decision Fatigue:** The constant barrage of choices, big or small, can lead to decision fatigue, making it difficult to make effective choices when they truly matter.

Decluttering Your Mental Landscape:

Here's how to create a mental haven that fosters focus, clarity, and well-being:

- **Embrace Mindfulness:** Mindfulness practices like meditation and deep breathing help you become aware of your thoughts and emotions without judgment. Focusing on the present moment reduces mental chatter and promotes calmness.

- **Brain Dump:** Externalize your worries and tasks by creating a comprehensive list of everything on your mind. Writing it down frees up mental space and allows you to categorize and prioritize later.

- **Prioritize Ruthlessly:** Utilize the Eisenhower Matrix to categorize tasks based on urgency and importance. Focus on completing high-impact tasks first and delegate, eliminate, or schedule less crucial activities.

- **Embrace Automation:** Technology can be your ally. Utilize tools like project management software, calendar apps, and to-do list applications to organize your tasks and deadlines, freeing up mental space for more complex thinking.

- **Schedule Time for "Decluttering":** Just like your physical workspace, your mind needs regular decluttering. Dedicate specific times for activities like planning, reviewing your to-do list, and addressing lingering worries.

- **Learn to Say No:** Don't be afraid to politely decline additional tasks or requests that don't align with your priorities or capacity. Saying no to the unimportant frees up space for the truly important.

- **Practice Gratitude:** Focusing on what you're grateful for can shift your mindset away from worries and anxieties. Gratitude practices can improve your overall well-being and mental clarity.

- **Get Enough Sleep:** Quality sleep is essential for mental health and cognitive function. Aim for 7-8 hours of sleep per night to allow your brain to rest, recharge, and process information effectively.

- **Move Your Body:** Regular exercise is a powerful tool for managing stress and improving cognitive function. Physical activity also helps to clear your head and promote mental clarity.

- **Embrace a Minimalist Mindset:** Consider applying minimalism to your physical space and digital life. Decluttering your surroundings can have a positive impact on mental clutter as well.

Building Habits for a Clearer Mind

Decluttering your mind is an ongoing process. Here are some habits to cultivate a culture of mental clarity:

- **Maintain a Journal:** Regular journaling allows you to process thoughts and emotions, identify recurring themes, and gain clarity on your priorities.

- **Practice Digital Detox:** Schedule regular breaks from technology to disconnect and allow your mind to unwind.

- **Spend Time in Nature:** Immersing yourself in nature has been shown to reduce stress, improve focus, and enhance creativity.

- **Prioritize Relaxation Techniques:** Find healthy ways to manage stress, such as yoga, deep breathing exercises, or spending time in hobbies you enjoy.

- **Learn to Forgive Yourself:** Don't dwell on past mistakes or disappointments. Forgive yourself and move forward with a clear mind.

Decluttering your mind is an investment in your overall well-being and success. By implementing these strategies and developing habits that promote mental clarity, you can free up valuable mental space, enhance your focus, and unlock your full potential. Remember, a clear mind is a powerful mind, ready to tackle any challenge and achieve remarkable things.

The Pomodoro Technique

Conquer Complexity: Maximizing Concentration with Short Work Intervals and Breaks

In our fast-paced world, maintaining focus can feel like a constant battle. Deadlines loom, distractions abound, and the allure of multitasking beckons. But what if the key to maximizing concentration wasn't about powering through long stretches of work, but rather embracing **short work intervals and strategic breaks**? This guide explores the science behind this approach and equips you with powerful strategies to unlock peak focus and achieve greater productivity.

The Science of Short Bursts:

Our brains aren't designed for sustained focus. Studies show that prolonged concentration leads to cognitive fatigue and decreased performance. Here's how short work intervals benefit your brain:

- **Enhanced Focus:** Short bursts of work allow you to enter a state of "flow," where distractions fade away and you're fully engaged in the task at hand.

- **Improved Information Processing:** Brief work intervals followed by breaks allow your brain to process information more effectively, leading to higher quality work and fewer errors.

- **Reduced Stress and Fatigue:** Constant focus leads to mental exhaustion. Short breaks provide a mental reset, preventing burnout and promoting sustained focus throughout the day.

The Power of the Pomodoro Technique

The Pomodoro Technique is a time management method that utilizes short work intervals and breaks. Here's how it works:

- **Set a Timer:** Choose a work interval duration (typically 25 minutes) and set a timer.

- **Focus on a Single Task:** Dedicate the entire interval to a single, well-defined task, minimizing distractions.

- **Take a Short Break:** When the timer rings, take a short break (typically 5 minutes) to refresh your mind.

- **Repeat and Reward:** Repeat this process for several intervals, followed by a longer break (15-30 minutes). After completing a set of Pomodoros (typically 4), reward yourself for maintaining focus.

Crafting Your Ideal Work Interval

The ideal work interval duration can vary depending on the individual and the task at hand. Here's how to find your sweet spot:

- **Experiment with Different Durations:** Start with shorter intervals (20-25 minutes) and gradually increase the length as you build focus stamina.

- **Consider Task Complexity:** More complex tasks may require shorter intervals to avoid overwhelm. Simple, repetitive tasks can benefit from slightly longer intervals.

- **Listen to Your Body:** Pay attention to your energy levels. If your focus starts to wane, take a break even if the timer hasn't gone off.

Maximizing Your Breaks

Breaks are not just about resting your mind. Use them strategically to enhance focus for the next interval:

- **Step Away from Your Desk:** Get some physical movement – stretch, walk around, or do some light exercise.

- **Engage in Mindful Activities:** Short meditation or deep breathing exercises can promote relaxation and refocus your attention.

- **Avoid Distractions:** Minimize exposure to screens and information overload during your breaks.

Beyond the Technique: Cultivating Focus-Friendly Habits

While the Pomodoro Technique is a powerful tool, consider these additional habits to maximize concentration throughout your day:

- **Prioritize ruthlessly:** Focus on the most important tasks and allocate dedicated work intervals for them. Delegate or eliminate less crucial activities.

- **Minimize multitasking:** Focus on completing one task at a time. Multitasking divides attention and hinders productivity.

- **Designate a Focus Zone:** Create a work environment that minimizes distractions. Declutter your desk, silence notifications, and consider noise-canceling headphones.

- **Schedule Breaks in Advance:** Don't wait until you're exhausted to take a break. Schedule them into your workday as a crucial part of maintaining focus.

- **Get Enough Sleep:** Aim for 7-8 hours of quality sleep each night. Adequate sleep is essential for maintaining cognitive function and focus.

- **Stay Hydrated:** Dehydration can significantly impact cognitive function. Drink plenty of water throughout the day to maintain focus and mental clarity.

- **Eat Nutritiously:** Fuel your brain with nutritious foods that provide sustained energy. Avoid sugary snacks and processed foods that can lead to energy crashes and decreased focus.

Embracing short work intervals and strategic breaks isn't a sign of weakness; it's a sign of understanding how your brain works best. By implementing these strategies and tailoring them to your individual needs, you can transform your work style, maximize concentration, and achieve remarkable results. Remember, focused work, punctuated by refreshing breaks, is the key to unlocking peak productivity and conquering complexity.

Conquering Fatigue: Maintaining Peak Performance Despite Feeling Drained

Fatigue is a relentless foe in the battle for productivity. Whether it stems from a long workweek, a lack of sleep, or simply the demands of daily life, feeling drained can significantly impact your ability to focus, complete tasks, and achieve your goals. But fear not, warriors of productivity! This guide equips you with powerful strategies to **combat fatigue and maintain peak performance** even when your energy levels dip.

The Multifaceted Monster: Understanding Fatigue

Fatigue isn't a one-size-fits-all feeling. It can manifest in various ways, impacting your physical, mental, and emotional well-being. Here's a breakdown of the different types of fatigue:

- **Physical Fatigue:** This manifests as muscle weakness, tiredness, and a lack of physical energy.

- **Mental Fatigue:** Difficulty concentrating, decreased alertness, and problems with memory and recall are signs of mental fatigue.

- **Emotional Fatigue:** Feeling emotionally drained, unmotivated, and lacking enthusiasm can be symptoms of emotional fatigue.

Identifying the Root Cause: The Key to Effective Solutions

To effectively combat fatigue, you need to understand its source. Common culprits include:

- **Sleep Deprivation:** Aim for 7-8 hours of quality sleep per night.

- **Stress:** Chronic stress can deplete energy levels. Practice stress management techniques like meditation or exercise.

- **Poor Diet:** Unhealthy eating habits lead to energy crashes. Focus on whole foods and stay hydrated.

- **Medical Conditions:** Certain medical conditions can cause fatigue. Consult a doctor if you suspect an underlying issue.

Combating Fatigue: A Multi-Pronged Approach

Here's your arsenal of strategies to fight fatigue and reclaim your energy:

- **Prioritize Sleep:** A good night's sleep is the foundation of sustained energy. Establish a regular sleep schedule and create a relaxing bedtime routine.

- **Fuel Your Body Right:** Nourish yourself with nutritious foods that provide sustained energy.

Focus on fruits, vegetables, whole grains, and lean protein.

- **Stay Hydrated:** Dehydration significantly impacts cognitive function and energy levels. Drink plenty of water throughout the day.

- **Move Your Body:** Regular exercise is a powerful tool for combating fatigue. Physical activity increases energy levels, improves sleep quality, and reduces stress.

- **Manage Stress:** Chronic stress is a major drain on your energy. Develop healthy stress management techniques like meditation, deep breathing exercises, or yoga.

- **Embrace Short Work Intervals:** Schedule dedicated work intervals with short breaks in between. The Pomodoro Technique (25 minutes of work followed by a 5-minute break) can be a powerful tool.

- **Minimize Distractions:** A cluttered workspace and constant notifications can drain your mental energy. Designate a focus zone and minimize distractions during work intervals.

- **Delegate and Eliminate:** Don't be a productivity martyr. Delegate or eliminate tasks that drain your energy and focus on high-impact activities.

- **Schedule Breaks Throughout the Day:** Get up and move around, stretch, or step outside for some fresh air. Planned breaks are essential for preventing burnout and maintaining focus.

- **Prioritize Relaxation:** Schedule time for activities you enjoy, whether it's reading, spending time in nature, or socializing with loved ones. Relaxation helps to recharge your batteries and combat fatigue.

- **Listen to Your Body:** Don't push yourself to the point of exhaustion. Take breaks when needed and prioritize getting enough rest.

Building a Sustainable System for Energy Management

Combating fatigue is an ongoing process. Here are some habits to cultivate a culture of sustained energy:

- **Maintain a Regular Sleep Schedule:** Go to bed and wake up at consistent times, even on weekends.

- **Create a Relaxing Bedtime Routine:** Wind down before bed with calming activities like reading or taking a warm bath. Avoid screens for at least an hour before sleep.

- **Plan Healthy Meals and Snacks:** Meal prep or plan healthy meals and snacks in advance to avoid resorting to unhealthy options when you're tired.

- **Schedule Workouts:** Treat exercise like an important appointment and schedule it into your calendar.

- **Develop Healthy Stress Management Techniques:** Practice stress management techniques regularly, not just when you're feeling overwhelmed.

Fatigue is a formidable opponent, but you are not powerless. By implementing these strategies and making lifestyle changes that prioritize your well-being, you can combat fatigue, maintain peak performance, and achieve your goals. Remember, a well-rested and energized you is a productive and unstoppable force. So, take charge of your energy levels and conquer the day!

Harness the Power of Automation

Utilize Technology to Streamline Repetitive Tasks

Taming the Chaos: Essential Tools for Streamlining Your Workflow

In today's fast-paced world, staying organized and efficient can feel like an uphill battle. Your inbox overflows with emails, your calendar is a labyrinth of appointments, and managing projects can feel like juggling chainsaws. But fear not, weary warriors of productivity! There's a digital cavalry waiting to charge in – a trio of powerful tools designed to streamline your workflow and empower you to achieve more with less. This guide explores **email autoresponders, scheduling tools, and project management software**, equipping you with the knowledge to choose the right tools for your needs and conquer the chaos of a busy world.

Email Autoresponders: Setting Boundaries and Saving Time

What it is: An email autoresponder is a tool that automatically sends pre-written responses to incoming emails. This can be a lifesaver for managing communication expectations and saving valuable time.

Common Uses:

- **Out-of-Office Replies:** Inform contacts of your absence and when you expect to return.

- **Welcome Messages:** Send an automated welcome message to new subscribers or customers.

- **Frequently Asked Questions (FAQs):** Provide pre-written responses to common inquiries, freeing you from repetitive emails.

- **Follow-up Reminders:** Schedule automated follow-up emails to nudge contacts or gently remind them of outstanding tasks.

Benefits:

- **Improved Customer Service:** Ensures timely communication, even when you're unavailable.

- **Increased Efficiency:** Frees up time for more important tasks.

- **Consistency in Communication:** Provides a professional and consistent experience for all contacts.

Choosing the Right Email Autoresponder:

Consider the following factors when selecting an email autoresponder:

- **Features:** Identify the functionalities you need, such as autoresponder templates, scheduling options, or analytics.

- **Integration:** Ensure the autoresponder integrates seamlessly with your existing email provider.

- **Pricing:** Various options exist, from free plans with limited features to premium plans offering advanced functionalities.

Scheduling Tools: Taking Control of Your Time

What it is: Scheduling tools are digital calendars that allow you to manage appointments, meetings, and events efficiently.

Common Uses:

- **Appointment Scheduling:** Streamline the process of scheduling appointments with colleagues, clients, or customers.

- **Meeting Management:** Schedule meetings, send invites, manage RSVPs, and keep track of meeting details.

- **Deadline and Task Management:** Set deadlines for tasks, receive reminders, and keep track of your overall workload.

- **Resource Sharing:** Identify and manage resource availability to prevent scheduling conflicts.

Benefits:

- **Reduced Communication Hassles:** Eliminate the back-and-forth of finding a suitable time for meetings.

- **Improved Time Management:** Visualize your schedule, prioritize tasks, and avoid double-booking.

- **Enhanced Collaboration:** Share schedules, delegate tasks, and stay on the same page with your team.

Choosing the Right Scheduling Tool:

Consider the following factors when selecting a scheduling tool:

- **Ease of Use:** The interface should be intuitive and user-friendly.

- **Integration:** Ensure the tool integrates with your existing calendar and other productivity tools.

- **Features:** Identify the functionalities you need, such as appointment booking, meeting room reservation, or video conferencing capabilities.

- **Team Collaboration:** If you work in a team, consider how the tool facilitates collaboration and information sharing.

Project Management Software: Orchestrating Success

What it is: Project management software provides a centralized platform for planning, organizing, and tracking projects.

Common Uses:

- **Project Planning:** Define project goals, break them down into smaller tasks, and create a project timeline.

- **Task Management:** Assign tasks to team members, set deadlines, track progress, and collaborate on deliverables.

- **Resource Management:** Allocate resources effectively, identify potential bottlenecks, and ensure everyone has the tools they need.

- **Communication and Collaboration:** Facilitate communication within the team, share files, and keep everyone on the same page.

Benefits:

- **Improved Project Visibility:** Gain a clear overview of project progress, identify roadblocks, and adjust plans as needed.

- **Enhanced Collaboration:** Facilitate communication and teamwork, keeping everyone informed and aligned.

- **Increased Efficiency:** Streamline workflows, manage resources effectively, and meet deadlines consistently.

- **Improved Project Outcomes:** Increase project success rates by identifying and mitigating potential issues proactively.

Choosing the Right Project Management Software:

With a plethora of options available, selecting the right tools can be overwhelming. Here are some tips to guide your decision:

- **Identify Your Needs:** Analyze your workflow and communication challenges. What specific problems are you trying to solve?

- **Research and Compare:** Explore available options and compare features, user reviews, and pricing models.

- **Start with Free Trials:** Many tools offer free trials. Utilize these trials to test functionality and user experience before committing financially.

- **Consider Integration:** Choose tools that integrate seamlessly with your existing software and workflow for optimal efficiency.

Email autoresponders, scheduling tools, and project management software are not magic bullets, but rather powerful allies in your quest for productivity. By implementing these tools and choosing the right ones for your specific needs, you can streamline communication, optimize scheduling, and manage projects with greater efficiency, allowing you to focus on what matters most – achieving your goals. Remember, the right tools, coupled with smart strategies, can empower you to conquer the chaos and thrive in today's fast-paced world.

Reclaim Your Time: Freeing Up Hours for What Truly Matters

Do you ever feel like there just aren't enough hours in the day? The to-do list seems endless, and the pressure to be productive mounts. But what if the answer to achieving more wasn't working harder, but working smarter? This guide equips you with powerful strategies to **free up time for high-value activities** that propel you towards your goals and leave you feeling fulfilled.

The High-Value Trap: Prioritizing the Right Activities

Not all tasks are created equal. Many activities, while seemingly productive, offer minimal value in the grand scheme of things. Here's how to identify high-value activities and delegate, eliminate, or automate the rest:

- **The Eisenhower Matrix:** Categorize tasks based on urgency and importance. Focus on completing high-impact, urgent tasks first and delegate, eliminate, or schedule less crucial activities.

- **The 80/20 Rule (Pareto Principle):** Identify the 20% of tasks that yield 80% of the results. Focus on those high-impact activities and consider outsourcing or eliminating the remaining 80%.

Identifying Time Wasters:

Be honest with yourself about where your time goes. Here are some common time wasters to watch out for:

- **Multitasking:** Contrary to popular belief, multitasking hinders productivity. Focus on completing one task at a time.

- **Social Media:** Set boundaries for social media use. Schedule short breaks to check in, but avoid getting sucked into an endless scroll.

- **Meetings:** Question the necessity of every meeting. If you can achieve the same outcome with an email or quick call, politely decline the invite.

- **Perfectionism:** Striving for perfection can lead to procrastination and wasted time. Aim for "good enough" and move on.

- **Disorganization:** A cluttered workspace and disorganized digital life can significantly eat into your productivity. Invest in organization systems and declutter your work environment.

Strategies for Time Reclamation:

Here are actionable steps to reclaim your time and dedicate it to what truly matters:

- **Embrace Automation:** Utilize technology to automate repetitive tasks. Explore email autoresponders, project management software, or online tools to streamline data entry, scheduling, or basic design tasks.

- **Batch Similar Tasks:** Group similar tasks together to minimize context switching. For example, dedicate specific times to respond to emails, return phone calls, or review reports.

- **Schedule Breaks:** Schedule regular breaks throughout the day to prevent burnout. Step away from your desk, stretch, or take a walk to refresh your mind and return to your work with renewed focus.

- **Learn to Say No:** Don't be afraid to politely decline additional tasks or requests that don't align with your priorities or capacity. Saying no to the unimportant frees up space for the truly important.

- **Delegate Effectively:** If possible, delegate tasks to colleagues or assistants. This frees up your time to focus on high-value activities requiring your specific expertise.

- **Outsource When Possible:** Consider outsourcing non-essential tasks to free up your time for core activities.

Creating Habits for Sustainable Time Management:

Freeing up time for high-value activities is a continuous process. Here are some habits to cultivate a culture of time management:

- **Maintain a Daily Schedule:** Plan your day in advance, allocating specific times for high-value activities.

- **Track Your Time:** Track your time for a few days to identify areas where your time is being spent and where you can make adjustments.

- **Review and Refine:** Regularly review your schedule and time management strategies. Be flexible and adapt your approach as needed.

- **Reward Yourself:** Acknowledge and reward yourself for completing high-value tasks and sticking to your time management plan.

By implementing these strategies and making conscious choices about how you spend your time, you can reclaim precious hours and dedicate them to activities that truly matter. Remember, time is your most valuable asset. Invest it wisely in activities that propel you towards your goals and leave you feeling fulfilled. Reclaim your time, and watch your productivity and well-being soar.

Leverage Templates and Presets

Build Once, Use Forever: Creating Reusable Templates for Invoices, Proposals, and Emails

Feeling bogged down by repetitive tasks? Creating invoices, proposals, and emails from scratch can be a significant time drain. But what if you could leverage the power of templates, crafting professional documents and communications in a fraction of the time? This guide equips you with strategies to **create reusable templates for invoices, proposals, and emails**, freeing up your time to focus on more strategic work.

The Power of Templates: Efficiency and Consistency

Templates offer a multitude of benefits:

- **Increased Efficiency:** Say goodbye to starting from scratch. Templates provide a pre-built framework, allowing you to quickly customize and generate documents and emails.

- **Enhanced Consistency:** Templates ensure a professional and consistent brand image across all your communications.

- **Reduced Errors:** Pre-populated templates minimize the risk of typos or missing information.

- **Improved Client Experience:** Streamlined communication and faster delivery of documents enhance the client experience.

Crafting Effective Templates: A Step-by-Step Guide

Here's a breakdown of how to create reusable templates for invoices, proposals, and emails:

Invoices:

- **Essential Information:** Include your company name, contact details, invoice number, date, client name, billing address, and a clear breakdown of services rendered, including descriptions, quantities, and unit prices.

- **Payment Details:** Specify payment terms, due date, and preferred payment methods (e.g., bank transfer, online payment portal).

- **Branding:** Incorporate your company logo and color scheme for a professional look.

- **Customization Options:** Create separate templates for different service categories or price structures.

Proposals:

- **Executive Summary:** Briefly introduce your company, the project scope, and the value proposition.

- **Problem and Solution:** Clearly define the client's challenge and how your services address it.

- **Proposed Methodology:** Outline your approach, including timelines, milestones, and key deliverables.

- **Experience and Qualifications:** Showcase your expertise and relevant past projects to inspire confidence.

- **Call to Action:** Clearly outline the next steps for the client and a compelling call to action.

- **Customization Options:** Create templates for different proposal types or client industries.

Emails:

- **Subject Line:** Craft a clear and concise subject line that accurately reflects the email's content.

- **Greeting:** Personalize the greeting with the recipient's name whenever possible.

- **Body:** Structure your email with a clear introduction, body text, and call to action. Use professional and concise language.

- **Signature Block:** Include your name, title, company name, contact details, and website URL.

- **Customization Options:** Create separate templates for common email purposes (e.g., follow-ups, welcome messages, thank-you notes).

Optimizing Your Templates for Different Platforms:

- **Software Compatibility:** Ensure your templates are compatible with your preferred invoice generation software, proposal software, or email marketing platform.

- **Formatting:** Optimize the formatting for easy reading across different devices (desktop, mobile).

- **Variable Fields:** Utilize placeholders or merge fields to easily insert dynamic information like client names, invoice numbers, or specific project details.

Building a Template Library:

Create a central repository for your templates to ensure easy access and maintain consistency across your team. Consider cloud-based storage solutions or project management platforms for easy collaboration.

Pro Tips for Template Success

- **Maintain a Professional Look:** Use high-quality fonts, consistent formatting, and clear visuals (if applicable).

- **Proofread Carefully:** Even templates need careful proofreading before they are sent out.

- **Update Regularly:** Review and update your templates periodically to reflect any changes in your business information or branding.

- **Share with Your Team:** If you work with a team, share your templates with colleagues to ensure everyone is sending out consistent communication.

Creating reusable templates doesn't have to be a daunting task. By following these steps and investing some time upfront, you can reap the benefits of efficiency, consistency, and a more streamlined workflow. Remember, templates are powerful tools that can free up your time and empower you to focus on what truly matters – growing your business and achieving your goals.

Streamlining Your Workflow: Eliminating Redundant Work and Boosting Efficiency

Feeling overwhelmed by a never-ending to-do list? Do you find yourself repeating the same tasks over and over again? You're not alone. Redundant work is a major time drain, hindering productivity and zapping your motivation. But fear not, efficiency warriors! This guide equips you with powerful strategies to **eliminate redundant work and enhance your overall workflow**.

The Burden of Redundancy: Understanding the Problem

Redundant work involves unnecessary repetition of tasks, leading to wasted time and reduced productivity. Here's how it impacts your workflow:

- **Decreased Efficiency:** Time spent on repetitive tasks steals away energy for more strategic work.

- **Increased Errors:** Repetitive tasks can lead to complacency and a higher probability of errors.

- **Reduced Motivation:** Doing the same thing repeatedly can be tedious and demotivating.

- **Hindered Innovation:** Focusing on routine tasks leaves less mental space for creative problem-solving and innovation.

Identifying Redundant Work:

The first step to eliminating redundancy is identifying it. Here are some areas to examine:

- **Administrative Tasks:** Streamline repetitive administrative tasks like data entry with automation or pre-filled forms.

- **Communication Channels:** Consolidate communication channels and avoid duplicating information across emails, meetings, and instant messaging platforms.

- **Meetings:** Question the necessity of every meeting. Can the information be effectively conveyed through email or a quick call?

- **Project Management:** Utilize project management tools to avoid duplicate efforts and ensure everyone is on the same page.

- **Software Usage:** Are you using multiple programs to achieve the same outcome? Consider consolidating your software use.

Strategies for Eliminating Redundancy:

Here are actionable steps to streamline your workflow and eliminate redundant work:

- **Embrace Automation:** Technology is your friend! Utilize tools for email autoresponders, scheduling, data entry, or project management to automate repetitive tasks.

- **Standardize Processes:** Develop clear and standardized procedures for frequently performed tasks to ensure consistency and efficiency.

- **Leverage Templates:** Create reusable templates for invoices, proposals, emails, and other commonly used documents. This saves time and ensures consistent formatting and branding.

- **Delegate Effectively:** Delegate appropriate tasks to team members based on their skills and expertise. This frees you up to focus on high-value activities.

- **Communicate Clearly:** Clear communication is key. Ensure everyone involved in a project understands their roles and responsibilities to avoid duplication of efforts.

- **Embrace Collaboration Tools:** Utilize project management platforms or collaboration tools to share information, assign tasks, and track progress in a centralized location.

- **Invest in Training:** Provide proper training to your team on the most efficient tools and processes to avoid time-wasting mistakes and ensure everyone is working effectively.

Cultivating a Culture of Efficiency:

Eliminating redundancy is an ongoing process. Here are some habits to cultivate a culture of efficiency:

- **Regularly Review Workflows:** Schedule time to review your workflows and identify areas for improvement.

- **Embrace Continuous Improvement:** Always be on the lookout for ways to streamline your processes and eliminate redundancy.

- **Encourage Feedback:** Seek feedback from colleagues and team members on ways to improve efficiency and eliminate unnecessary steps.

- **Measure and Analyze:** Track time spent on different tasks to identify areas where automation or delegation could be beneficial.

- **Reward Efficiency:** Acknowledge and reward team members who identify opportunities to eliminate redundancy and improve efficiency.

By eliminating redundant work and streamlining your workflow, you can reclaim precious time, boost your productivity, and achieve more with less effort. Remember, efficiency isn't about working harder; it's about working smarter. Embrace these strategies, cultivate a culture of continuous improvement, and watch your productivity soar!

Tame Your Inbox and Manage Communication

Unsubscribe from Unnecessary Emails and Newsletters

Conquering the Chaos: Reducing Distractions and Information Overload

In today's hyper-connected world, distractions and information overload are constant threats to focus and productivity. A never-ending stream of notifications, social media updates, and email alerts can leave you feeling overwhelmed and unable to concentrate. But fear not, warriors of focus! This guide equips you with powerful strategies to **reduce distractions and information overload**, empowering you to reclaim your attention and achieve peak performance.

The Duality of Information: A Blessing and a Curse

Information is a powerful tool, but it can also be a double-edged sword. Here's how information overload impacts us:

- **Decreased Focus:** Constant distractions fragment attention and make it difficult to concentrate on deep work.

- **Decision Fatigue:** Making too many choices throughout the day depletes your mental resources, leading to poor decision-making.

- **Increased Stress and Anxiety:** The feeling of being overwhelmed by information can trigger stress and anxiety.

- **Reduced Creativity:** Constant information intake leaves little space for creative thinking and problem-solving.

Identifying Your Distractions

The first step to reducing distractions is understanding what distracts you. Here are some common culprits:

- **Digital Distractions:** Notifications from email, social media, and messaging apps can significantly disrupt focus.

- **Physical Environment:** Clutter, noise, and uncomfortable workspaces can hinder concentration.

- **Internal Distractions:** Worry, stress, and unresolved personal issues can pull your focus away from the task at hand.

Strategies for a Distraction-Free Zone

Here's your arsenal of weapons to combat distractions and reclaim your focus:

- **Digital Detox:** Schedule regular breaks from technology. Silence notifications, put your phone away, and focus on the task at hand.

- **Utilize Focus Tools:** Explore browser extensions or apps that block distracting websites and social media platforms.

- **Designate a Focus Zone:** Create a dedicated workspace that is free from clutter and distractions.

- **Embrace the Power of Silence:** Minimize background noise by wearing noise-canceling headphones or working in a quiet environment.

- **Practice Mindfulness:** Mindfulness techniques like meditation can help you become more aware of distractions and refocus your attention.

- **Single-Tasking is King:** Focus on completing one task at a time. Multitasking is a myth that leads to errors and decreased efficiency.

- **Schedule Time for Distractions:** Allocate specific times to check emails, social media, or make personal calls. This prevents them from interrupting your deep work periods.

Taming the Information Beast: Strategies for Content Consumption

Here's how to manage information overload and consume information mindfully:

- **Unsubscribe Mercilessly:** Ruthlessly unsubscribe from emails and information sources that no longer serve you.

- **Curate Your News Feed:** Unfollow irrelevant accounts and social media groups that contribute to information overload.

- **Prioritize High-Quality Sources:** Focus on credible and reliable sources for information.

- **Schedule Information Consumption:** Dedicate specific times for reading articles, checking news updates, or browsing social media.

- **Embrace the Power of Summary:** Utilize tools that provide summaries of lengthy articles or news stories.

- **Practice Active Reading:** Don't passively consume information. Actively engage with the content, take notes, and ask questions.

- **Embrace Offline Learning:** Sometimes, the best way to learn is by stepping away from screens altogether. Consider reading physical books or listening to audiobooks.

Building Habits for Sustainable Focus

Reducing distractions and managing information overload is an ongoing process. Here are some habits to cultivate a culture of focus:

- **Establish a Routine:** Create a consistent daily routine for work and information consumption.

- **Plan Your Day:** Start your day by prioritizing tasks and scheduling time for deep work sessions.

- **Take Regular Breaks:** Schedule short breaks throughout the day to prevent burnout and refresh your mind.

- **Reward Yourself:** Acknowledge and reward yourself for staying focused and completing tasks.

- **Communicate Your Needs:** Inform colleagues and family about your focus times and request they respect your need for distraction-free work periods.

In today's information age, protecting your focus is a crucial skill. By implementing these strategies and cultivating a culture of mindful information consumption, you can reclaim your attention, conquer distractions, and achieve remarkable results. Remember, a focused mind is a productive mind. So, silence the distractions, tame the information beast, and unleash your full potential!

Inbox Avalanche: Prioritizing Emails That Impact Your Income

The email notification dings. Another email. Another to-do. But wait, is this email crucial for your income, or just another piece of digital clutter? In today's fast-paced world, our inboxes overflow with messages, and the ability to prioritize effectively is essential. This guide equips you with powerful strategies to **prioritize emails that impact your income**, ensuring you stay on top of critical communications and maximize your earning potential.

The Cost of a Disorganized Inbox:

A cluttered and unorganized inbox can have significant consequences for your income:

- **Missed Opportunities:** Important business inquiries or potential collaborations might get buried under a mountain of emails.

- **Delayed Responses:** Clients or partners might perceive a slow response as unprofessionalism, impacting future opportunities.

- **Reduced Productivity:** Constantly checking and sorting through emails can significantly disrupt your focus and workflow.

- **Increased Stress:** The feeling of being overwhelmed by an overflowing inbox can be a major source of stress.

Identifying Income-Impacting Emails

Not all emails are created equal. Here's how to identify messages that directly or indirectly impact your income:

- **Client Communication:** This includes emails from existing clients regarding project updates, revisions, or new project inquiries.

- **Sales Inquiries:** Emails from potential clients expressing interest in your services or products are crucial for income generation.

- **Financial Communications:** Invoices, payment confirmations, and tax-related emails all have a direct bearing on your finances.

- **Partnership Opportunities:** Emails proposing collaborations, joint ventures, or affiliate marketing opportunities can be significant income drivers.

- **Industry Updates:** Information on market trends, competitor activity, or new technologies can impact your earning potential.

Strategies for Prioritization Prowess

Here's your arsenal of email management techniques to ensure you don't miss income-critical messages:

- **Utilize Labels and Folders:** Create custom labels or folders for different categories of emails, such as "Client Communication," "Sales Inquiries," and "Financial."

- **Implement Filters:** Set up filters to automatically move income-related emails to designated folders, saving you time sorting through your inbox.

- **Prioritize High-Impact Messages:** Start your day by reviewing your prioritized folders and addressing high-impact emails first.

- **Flagging and Starring:** Flag or star important emails to ensure you don't lose track of them in the daily flood of messages.

- **Utilize Importance Markers:** Many email services offer "Important" or "Starred" markers. Use them strategically to highlight income-critical messages.

- **Schedule Follow-Up Reminders:** For critical emails requiring action, set reminders to ensure you follow up promptly.

- **Leverage Canned Responses:** Create pre-written responses for common inquiries to save time and ensure consistent communication.

Advanced Tactics for the Inbox Master

Here are some additional strategies to further streamline your email management:

- **Unsubscribe Mercilessly:** Unsubscribe from irrelevant mailing lists and promotional emails that contribute to inbox clutter.

- **Explore Automation Tools:** Consider email automation tools that can handle routine tasks like sending follow-up emails or appointment reminders.

- **Leverage Search Functionality:** Master the search function in your email client to quickly locate specific messages when needed.

- **Schedule Email Checking Times:** Allocate specific times throughout the day to check your emails. Avoid constantly checking your inbox, which can disrupt focus.

- **Mobile Management:** Utilize the mobile app for your email client to stay connected on the go and address urgent income-related messages promptly.

Building Habits for Inbox Efficiency

Mastering your inbox is an ongoing process. Here are some habits to cultivate long-term email management success:

- **Maintain a Clean Inbox:** At the end of your workday, strive to have a zero-inbox or a minimal number of remaining messages.

- **Review Your System Regularly:** Periodically review your email management system, including labels, filters, and rules, to ensure optimal efficiency.

- **Communicate Your Expectations:** Inform clients and partners about your preferred communication methods and response times.

- **Delegate When Possible:** If your inbox workload becomes overwhelming, consider delegating email management tasks to a virtual assistant or team member.

Your inbox shouldn't be a source of stress or missed opportunities. By implementing these strategies and making deliberate choices about how you manage your email, you can transform your inbox into a powerful tool that fuels your earning potential. Remember, a well-organized inbox leads to a clear mind and a maximized income stream. So, take control of your inbox, and watch your income flourish!

Batch Processing Emails

Taming the Multitasking Myth: Minimizing Context Switching and Streamlining Communication

In our hyper-connected world, we juggle a constant barrage of notifications, emails, and messages. We jump from task to task, feeling like we're constantly catching up, never truly focused. This constant **context switching** – the mental shift between different tasks – is a productivity killer. But fear not, warriors of efficiency! This guide equips you with powerful strategies to **minimize context switching and streamline communication management**, empowering you to reclaim your focus and achieve more with less.

The High Cost of Context Switching:

The impact of context switching goes beyond feeling overwhelmed. Here's how it hinders your productivity:

- **Reduced Focus:** Each time you switch tasks, it takes time to refocus and regain your mental state.

- **Increased Errors:** Jumping between tasks can lead to mistakes and oversights.

- **Decreased Productivity:** The constant mental shift fragments your attention, hindering your ability to complete tasks efficiently.

- **Increased Stress and Frustration:** The feeling of being pulled in a million directions can be a significant source of stress and frustration.

Identifying Context Switches:

The first step to minimizing context switching is understanding where it occurs. Here are some common culprits:

- **Multitasking:** Contrary to popular belief, multitasking hinders efficiency. Focus on completing one task at a time.

- **Constant Notifications:** Email alerts, social media pings, and phone notifications can disrupt your focus and pull you away from your current task.

- **Open Communication Channels:** Being available on multiple platforms (email, instant messaging, phone calls) can lead to distractions and context switching.

- **Unplanned Interruptions:** Colleagues dropping by your desk or unexpected phone calls can significantly disrupt your workflow.

Strategies for Minimized Context Switching

Here's your arsenal of techniques to combat context switching and maintain focus:

- **Batch Similar Tasks:** Group similar tasks together to minimize context switching. For example, dedicate specific times to respond to emails, return calls, or review reports.

- **Embrace the Power of "Do Not Disturb":** Utilize "Do Not Disturb" modes on your phone and computer to block notifications during deep work sessions.

- **Schedule Communication Checkpoints:** Dedicate specific times throughout the day to check emails, messages, and voicemails.

- **Communicate Your Needs:** Inform colleagues and clients about your preferred communication methods and preferred times for availability.

- **Embrace Asynchronous Communication:** Utilize tools like project management platforms or task management software for asynchronous communication, allowing others to reach you without immediate interruption.

- **Schedule Meetings Strategically:** Consolidate meetings and schedule them at designated times to avoid disrupting your workflow.

Streamlining Communication Management

Effective communication is crucial, but it shouldn't come at the expense of your focus. Here's how to streamline communication:

- **Utilize the Right Tools:** Choose the appropriate communication channel for the message. Urgent matters might require a phone call, while project updates can be communicated via email or project management software.

- **Set Communication Expectations:** Inform your team about preferred communication methods and response times for different types of inquiries.

- **Leverage Collaboration Tools:** Utilize project management platforms with built-in communication features to centralize discussions and avoid email overload.

- **Embrace Templates:** Create pre-written templates for common responses to inquiries or project updates to save time and ensure consistent communication.

Cultivating Habits for Sustainable Focus

Minimizing context switching and streamlining communication is an ongoing process. Here are some habits to cultivate a culture of focused work:

- **Plan Your Day:** Schedule your tasks for the day, allocating specific time blocks for deep work sessions and communication check-ins.

- **Take Regular Breaks:** Schedule short breaks throughout the day to prevent burnout and refresh your mind.

- **Reward Yourself:** Acknowledge and reward yourself for staying focused and completing tasks efficiently.

- **Review and Refine:** Periodically review your communication management strategies and adjust them as needed to optimize your workflow.

By mastering the art of focus and prioritizing communication management, you can transform your work experience. Remember, focus is the key to unleashing your full potential. Implement these strategies, cultivate a culture of mindful communication, and watch your productivity soar. You'll be amazed at how much you can achieve when you're not constantly switching gears!

The Art of the Timely Response: Utilizing Scheduling Features to Maximize Impact

In today's fast-paced world, effective communication is paramount. But timing is just as crucial as the message itself. A well-crafted email sent at the wrong time might get buried in an inbox avalanche, while a follow-up call during a busy meeting can be disruptive and unproductive. This guide dives into the power of **scheduling features** – your secret weapon for **responding at optimal times**, maximizing the impact of your communication and boosting your overall workflow.

The Power of Timing: Why It Matters

The timing of your communication can significantly impact its effectiveness:

- **Increased Visibility:** Sending emails during peak email usage hours increases the chances of your message getting noticed.

- **Improved Response Rates:** Matching your response time to the urgency of the message sets clear expectations and encourages timely replies.

- **Enhanced Customer Experience:** Responding promptly conveys professionalism and respect for the recipient's time.

- **Reduced Back-and-forth Communication:** Scheduling follow-up emails can ensure your message doesn't get lost and reduces the need for repetitive inquiries.

Understanding Scheduling Features

Many communication and project management tools offer scheduling features that can transform your workflow. Here's a breakdown of some key functionalities:

- **Email Scheduling:** Compose your email in advance and schedule it to be sent at a specific time or date. This allows you to craft thoughtful messages at your convenience and deliver them when the recipient is most likely to be receptive.

- **Meeting Scheduling:** Schedule meetings with colleagues or clients by proposing time slots through integrated calendars. This streamlines communication and eliminates the tedious back-and-forth of finding a suitable time.

- **Follow-up Reminders:** Schedule automatic follow-up emails to nudge recipients who haven't responded to your initial message. This ensures your message doesn't get lost and keeps the conversation moving forward.

- **Time Zone Synchronization:** Schedule communication considering different time zones to avoid sending emails at inconvenient hours for the recipient.

Strategies for Optimal Timing

Here's your arsenal of tactics to leverage scheduling features for impactful communication:

- **Research Recipient Habits:** Consider the recipient's typical work hours and email usage patterns to schedule your message for optimal visibility.

- **Prioritize Urgency:** Schedule urgent messages for delivery during peak work hours (within reason) to ensure prompt attention.

- **Schedule Follow-Ups Strategically:** Set follow-up emails to arrive one or two days after your initial message, providing enough time for a response without appearing pushy.

- **Plan for Different Time Zones:** Utilize time zone synchronization features to schedule messages for a convenient time in the recipient's location.

- **Leverage Automated Features:** Take advantage of auto-scheduling for recurring emails or follow-ups, freeing up your time for more strategic tasks.

Beyond Email: Scheduling for All Communication Channels:

Scheduling features extend beyond email:

- **Calendar Scheduling:** Utilize calendar apps to schedule meetings, calls, or video conferences at times convenient for everyone involved.

- **Task Management Tools:** Schedule deadlines and reminders within project management platforms for team collaboration and clear expectations on response times.

- **Social Media Management:** Schedule social media posts for optimal engagement times based on your target audience's location and online behavior.

Building Habits for Time-Conscious Communication:

Making the most of scheduling features is an ongoing process. Here are some habits to cultivate:

- **Plan Your Communication:** Allocate specific times in your schedule for composing and sending emails or scheduling calls.

- **Review Analytics:** Utilize email analytics tools or social media insights to understand peak engagement times for your audience.

- **Set Communication Expectations:** Inform colleagues, clients, and collaborators about your preferred communication channels and response timelines.

- **Refine Your Approach:** Regularly review your scheduling strategies and adapt them as needed based on your communication needs and goals.

By mastering the art of timing and leveraging scheduling features, you can elevate your communication to a whole new level. Remember, timely communication is a powerful tool that builds trust, fosters collaboration, and drives results. So, embrace scheduling features, respond at optimal times, and watch your communication impact soar!

Learn to Say No (Without Feeling Guilty)

Identify Projects and Requests That Drain Your Time and Resources

The Art of Saying No: Recognizing Opportunities That Don't Align with Your Income Goals

In the pursuit of success, it's easy to get caught up in the whirlwind of "yes." Every opportunity seems like a step forward, a chance to climb the ladder. But what if some opportunities are actually holding you back from achieving your true income goals? This guide equips you with the skills to **recognize opportunities that don't align with your income goals**, empowering you to make strategic choices and maximize your earning potential.

The Duality of Opportunity: Not All Shine Is Gold

Not every opportunity is created equal. Here's why some projects might not be the best fit for your income goals:

- **Low Pay Rate:** The offered compensation might not be enough to justify the time and effort invested.

- **Scope Creep:** The initial project scope may expand, leading to additional workload without a corresponding increase in pay.

- **Unstructured Payment Terms:** Unclear or delayed payment terms can disrupt your cash flow and create financial uncertainty.

- **Hidden Costs:** The project might have hidden costs, such as required software subscriptions or travel expenses, eating into your net income.

- **Long-Term Commitment:** A long-term project with a low initial payout might not be the best choice if you need to generate income quickly.

Identifying Misaligned Opportunities:

The first step to making strategic choices is understanding what to look for. Here are some red flags to watch out for:

- **Unclear Project Scope:** A project with an undefined scope or constantly changing requirements can lead to unexpected work and difficulty in accurately estimating income.

- **Focus on "Exposure" Over Pay:** Opportunities that prioritize exposure over fair compensation might not be financially sustainable in the long run.

- **Unrealistic Deadlines:** Extremely tight deadlines might necessitate sacrificing quality or working long hours, potentially leading to burnout and impacting future earning potential.

- **Unreliable Clients:** A history of late payments or bad business practices from a client can create financial strain and hinder your income goals.

- **Gut Feeling:** Sometimes, you just have a bad feeling about an opportunity. Trust your intuition and don't ignore red flags.

Strategies for Saying No Gracefully:

Declining an opportunity can be tricky. Here's how to do it politely and professionally:

- **Express Gratitude:** Thank the potential client or collaborator for considering you.

- **Explain Your Reasons:** Be honest and transparent about why the opportunity doesn't align with your current goals or priorities.

- **Offer Alternatives:** If possible, suggest alternative solutions or suggest a referral if someone else might be a better fit.

- **Maintain a Positive Relationship:** End on a positive note, leaving the door open for future collaboration if circumstances change.

Building a Sustainable Income Stream:

Making informed choices about opportunities is crucial for long-term financial success. Here are some habits to cultivate:

- **Define Your Income Goals:** Clearly define your desired income level and preferred work structure.

- **Calculate Your Project Rates:** Factor in your time, expertise, and desired income when setting your project rates.

- **Diversify Your Income Streams:** Explore different income sources, such as consulting, freelance work, or passive income, to reduce reliance on any single opportunity.

- **Network Strategically:** Build relationships with potential clients who value your skills and are willing to compensate you fairly.

- **Invest in Yourself:** Continuously hone your skills and knowledge to increase your value proposition and command higher rates.

Saying no to misaligned opportunities isn't about being afraid to take risks; it's about making strategic choices that propel you towards your financial goals. By recognizing red flags and prioritizing opportunities that support your income needs, you can build a sustainable and fulfilling career path. Remember, your time and skills are valuable assets. Learn to say no strategically, and watch your income goals come into sharp focus!

The Power of "Enough": Setting Boundaries and Protecting Your Valuable Time

In today's constantly connected world, the lines between work and personal life can easily blur. We juggle overflowing to-do lists, relentless notifications, and a pervasive feeling of "never having enough time." But what if the key to regaining control lies in setting boundaries? This guide equips you with powerful strategies to **set clear boundaries and protect your valuable time**, empowering you to achieve a healthy work-life balance and reclaim your sanity.

The Erosion of Time: Why Boundaries Matter

Without clear boundaries, our time becomes a free-for-all, leading to:

- **Burnout:** Constantly saying "yes" to everything leads to exhaustion and hinders productivity.

- **Resentment:** Feeling overwhelmed and taken advantage of can breed resentment towards work and colleagues.

- **Reduced Effectiveness:** Being stretched too thin hinders your ability to focus and deliver your best work.

- **Increased Stress:** The constant pressure to be available can lead to chronic stress and anxiety.

- **Neglecting Personal Life:** Without boundaries, work can encroach on personal time, impacting relationships and well-being.

Understanding Boundaries: What They Are and Why They Work

Boundaries are imaginary lines we draw to define our personal space – physical, emotional, and mental. Here's why setting boundaries is crucial:

- **Increased Clarity:** Boundaries create clear expectations for yourself and others regarding your availability and workload.

- **Improved Work-Life Balance:** Boundaries establish a healthy separation between work and personal life, promoting overall well-being.

- **Reduced Stress:** Saying "no" to unreasonable demands eliminates unnecessary pressure and promotes peace of mind.

- **Enhanced Productivity:** Focusing on prioritized tasks within established boundaries leads to increased efficiency and effectiveness.

- **Stronger Relationships:** Boundaries create a foundation for respectful and healthy interactions with colleagues and clients.

Strategies for Setting Effective Boundaries:

Setting boundaries is a skill that takes practice. Here are some steps to get you started:

- **Identify Your Needs:** Reflect on your priorities, values, and energy levels. What do you need to feel fulfilled and productive?

- **Communicate Clearly:** Articulate your boundaries to colleagues, clients, and family. Be direct, honest, and respectful.

- **Practice Saying No:** Learn to politely decline requests that don't align with your priorities or time constraints.

- **Lead by Example:** Model healthy boundaries by respecting the boundaries of others.

- **Schedule Time for Yourself:** Block out time in your calendar for personal needs – relaxation, hobbies, or spending time with loved ones.

Tools and Techniques for Boundary Maintenance:

Here are some practical tools to help you uphold your boundaries:

- **Utilize Technology:** Leverage features like "Do Not Disturb" mode on your phone or email scheduling to manage your availability.

- **Create Dedicated Workspaces:** Designate a specific area for work, and avoid working in areas meant for relaxation.

- **Establish Communication Protocols:** Set clear expectations for response times for emails, calls, or messages outside of work hours.

- **Delegate Tasks:** Learn to delegate tasks when appropriate to avoid overwork and empower others.

- **Learn to Disengage:** Disconnect from work outside of designated working hours to avoid constant availability.

Building Habits for a Balanced Life:

Maintaining boundaries is an ongoing process. Here are some habits to cultivate a culture of self-respect and time management:

- **Regularly Review Your Boundaries:** As your needs and priorities evolve, revisit and adjust your boundaries accordingly.

- **Communicate Proactively:** Don't wait for burnout to set boundaries. Communicate your needs as situations arise.

- **Be Assertive, Not Aggressive:** Set boundaries with confidence and respect, but avoid being confrontational.

- **Reward Yourself:** Acknowledge and reward yourself for setting and upholding healthy boundaries.

- **Seek Support:** If you struggle to set boundaries, consider talking to a therapist or counselor for guidance.

Setting boundaries isn't selfish; it's self-care. By establishing clear boundaries and protecting your valuable time, you can reclaim control of your life, reduce stress, and achieve a healthy work-life balance. Remember, you are not defined by your work. Set boundaries, prioritize your well-being, and watch your productivity and overall life satisfaction soar!

Offer Alternative Solutions or Referrals When Appropriate

Balancing Act: Maintaining Positive Relationships While Prioritizing Your Workload

The professional world often presents a delicate balancing act: meeting deadlines, managing a heavy workload, and nurturing positive relationships with colleagues and clients. Neglecting either side of this equation can have consequences. This guide equips you with powerful strategies to **maintain positive relationships while prioritizing your workload**, fostering a supportive work environment and achieving success without sacrificing connections.

The Importance of Positive Relationships:

Strong relationships in the workplace go beyond just being friendly. Here's why they matter:

- **Enhanced Collaboration:** Positive relationships foster open communication, leading to better teamwork and problem-solving.

- **Increased Support:** A supportive network of colleagues can provide encouragement, feedback, and assistance during challenging times.

- **Improved Job Satisfaction:** Feeling valued and connected to others contributes to a more positive and fulfilling work experience.

- **Enhanced Reputation:** Being known for your positive and collaborative spirit can build trust and open doors to future opportunities.

The Workload Squeeze: How It Impacts Relationships

A heavy workload can strain workplace relationships in several ways:

- **Reduced Availability:** Long hours and tight deadlines can leave less time for casual conversations and fostering connections.

- **Increased Stress:** Feeling overwhelmed can lead to short tempers, strained communication, and a disconnect with colleagues.

- **Misunderstandings:** Without clear communication, colleagues might perceive your focus on work as dismissiveness or a lack of interest.

Strategies for Prioritizing Both Work and Relationships:

Here's your arsenal of tactics to navigate the workload-relationship tightrope:

- **Communicate Openly:** Inform colleagues and clients about your workload and deadlines. Set realistic expectations for response times.

- **Practice Time Management:** Utilize time management techniques to prioritize tasks and maximize your efficiency, allowing time for brief interactions.

- **Embrace Small Gestures:** Even small acts of kindness, like a quick hello or offering help, can go a long way in maintaining positive connections.

- **Schedule Social Time:** Dedicate time for informal interactions with colleagues, like team lunches or virtual coffee breaks.

- **Celebrate Successes:** Take time to acknowledge and celebrate both individual and team accomplishments. This fosters camaraderie and builds morale.

Leveraging Technology for Connection:

Technology can be a powerful tool for maintaining relationships in a busy work environment:

- **Utilize Communication Platforms:** Use instant messaging platforms for quick updates, questions, or informal conversations.

- **Team Building Activities:** Explore online team-building exercises or virtual social events to connect with colleagues remotely.

- **Recognition Tools:** Utilize company recognition platforms to acknowledge colleagues' achievements and publicly express appreciation.

- **Internal Social Media:** Participate in internal social media platforms to share personal updates and connect with colleagues outside of work-related topics.

Building Habits for Relationship Harmony:

Maintaining positive relationships at work is an ongoing process. Here are some habits to cultivate a culture of collaboration and support:

- **Be an Active Listener:** Pay attention to colleagues, take the time to understand their challenges, and offer support when possible.

- **Show Gratitude:** Express appreciation to colleagues for their contributions, both big and small.

- **Maintain a Positive Attitude:** A positive and approachable demeanor fosters a more pleasant and collaborative work environment.

- **Be Empathetic:** Try to see things from your colleagues' perspectives and be understanding of their needs and workloads.

- **Offer Help:** Proactively offer assistance to colleagues when you see them struggling.

Prioritizing your workload doesn't mean neglecting your relationships. By implementing these strategies and cultivating a culture of open communication and mutual support, you can achieve a healthy balance. Strong relationships at work can make even the most demanding tasks more manageable and enjoyable. Remember, success is not just about individual achievement; it's about working together and building a supportive network. So, prioritize your workload, nurture your relationships, and watch your career flourish in a positive and collaborative environment!

The Bedrock of Collaboration: Building Trust and Respect Through Open Communication

In today's dynamic work environments, effective communication is paramount. But true success hinges on more than just conveying information. It's about fostering trust and respect – the cornerstones of strong working relationships and a collaborative spirit. This guide explores the power of **open communication** and equips you with strategies to build trust and respect through your interactions.

The Power of Open Communication:

Open communication goes beyond simply exchanging information. It's about creating a space for honest dialogue, transparency, and mutual understanding. Here's why it matters:

- **Builds Trust:** Open communication fosters transparency and honesty, which are essential for building trust with colleagues and clients.

- **Enhances Respect:** Actively listening to others and valuing their perspectives demonstrates respect and creates a more inclusive environment.

- **Boosts Collaboration:** Open communication allows for a free flow of ideas, leading to better problem-solving and collaboration.

- **Reduces Conflict:** By addressing issues openly and honestly, misunderstandings and conflicts can be minimized.

- **Increases Engagement:** When employees feel comfortable expressing their opinions and concerns, they become more engaged and invested in their work.

Essential Elements of Open Communication:

Open communication is a two-way street. Here are the key elements:

- **Honesty and Transparency:** Be truthful and forthcoming in your communication, even when delivering difficult messages.

- **Active Listening:** Pay close attention to what others are saying, both verbally and nonverbally. Ask clarifying questions to demonstrate understanding.

- **Empathy:** Try to see things from the perspective of others and acknowledge their feelings.

- **Clear and Concise Communication:** Express yourself clearly and avoid jargon or ambiguity. Tailor your communication style to your audience.

- **Respectful Dialogue:** Even when disagreeing, maintain a respectful tone and avoid personal attacks.

Strategies for Fostering Open Communication:

Here are some practical tactics to cultivate an environment of open communication:

- **Hold Regular Team Meetings:** Schedule regular meetings to discuss projects, challenges, and ideas. Encourage open participation from all team members.

- **Implement Open-Door Policy:** Make yourself readily available for questions, concerns, or suggestions from colleagues.

- **Provide Feedback Channels:** Create anonymous or confidential channels for employees to provide feedback, both positive and negative.

- **Embrace Diverse Perspectives:** Encourage open dialogue and actively seek out different viewpoints for a more holistic understanding.

- **Celebrate Open Communication:** Recognize and acknowledge instances of open communication and transparency within your team.

Building Habits for Trust and Respect:

Open communication is an ongoing practice. Here are some habits to cultivate a culture of trust and respect:

- **Lead by Example:** Demonstrate open communication in your own interactions with colleagues and clients.

- **Be Approachable:** Maintain a positive and approachable demeanor to encourage others to come forward with ideas or concerns.

- **Practice Empathy:** Actively seek to understand the perspectives and challenges faced by your colleagues.

- **Acknowledge Mistakes:** Everyone makes mistakes. Be willing to admit yours and use them as learning opportunities.

- **Show Appreciation:** Express gratitude to colleagues for their contributions to foster a positive and respectful work environment.

Open communication isn't just about delivering information; it's about building relationships. By incorporating these strategies and fostering an environment of transparency and respect, you can unlock the true potential of your team. Remember, trust and respect are the foundations of a strong and successful workplace. Let open communication be the bridge that connects you all!

Embrace the Power of Outsourcing

Delegate Tasks That Others Can Do More Efficiently

Reclaim Your Time: Strategies to Focus on High-Impact Activities

In today's fast-paced world, our days seem to vanish in a blur of emails, meetings, and never-ending to-do lists. The crucial high-impact activities that drive progress often get pushed aside. But what if you could reclaim your time and dedicate it to the work that truly matters? This guide equips you with powerful strategies to **free up your time** and **focus on high-impact activities**, empowering you to achieve more with less.

The Time Crunch: Why It Matters

Feeling constantly overwhelmed by tasks can have a significant impact on your productivity and well-being:

- **Reduced Focus:** Juggling multiple tasks at once hinders your ability to focus deeply and deliver your best work.

- **Increased Stress:** The constant pressure to "do it all" can lead to chronic stress and burnout.

- **Missed Opportunities:** Neglecting high-impact activities can limit your career growth and hinder your ability to make a significant contribution.

- **Decreased Motivation:** The feeling of being overwhelmed can lead to a lack of motivation and decreased overall productivity.

Identifying Time-Wasters:

The first step to reclaiming your time is understanding where it goes. Here are some common culprits:

- **Multitasking:** Contrary to popular belief, multitasking hinders efficiency. Focus on one task at a time.

- **Unnecessary Meetings:** Evaluate the purpose and necessity of meetings. Can the information be communicated through email or asynchronous communication?

- **Social Media and Distractions:** Limit your time on social media and other distracting websites during work hours.

- **Cluttered Workspace:** A cluttered physical or digital workspace can hinder focus and make it difficult to find what you need.

- **Perfectionism:** Striving for perfection on every task can eat away at valuable time. Focus on getting things done well enough, not perfectly.

Strategies for Time Reclamation:

Here's your arsenal of techniques to reclaim your time and focus on what matters most:

- **Prioritize ruthlessly:** Identify the most important tasks (high-impact activities) that contribute directly to your goals.

- **Embrace the Power of "No":** Learn to politely decline requests that don't align with your priorities or time constraints.

- **Batch Similar Tasks:** Group similar tasks together to minimize context switching and improve efficiency.

- **Utilize the Pareto Principle (80/20 Rule):** Focus on the 20% of tasks that yield 80% of the results.

- **Delegate and Outsource:** Delegate tasks that can be done by others or outsource them when possible.

- **Schedule Time for High-Impact Activities:** Block time in your calendar specifically for high-impact activities and treat these time slots as sacred.

Tools and Techniques for Time Management:

Technology can be a powerful tool for managing your time effectively:

- **Time Management Apps:** Utilize time management apps to track your time, set goals, and schedule tasks.

- **Project Management Tools:** Project management tools can help you stay organized, collaborate with others, and track project progress.

- **Focus Tools:** Explore browser extensions or apps that block distracting websites for a set period of time.

- **Calendar Scheduling:** Utilize scheduling features in your calendar to prevent double bookings and manage your time effectively.

- **Automation Tools:** Consider automation tools for repetitive tasks, freeing up time for more strategic work.

Building Habits for Sustainable Efficiency:

Time management is an ongoing process. Here are some habits to cultivate a culture of focus and productivity:

- **Review Your Schedule Regularly:** Periodically review your schedule and adjust it as needed based on your priorities and workload.

- **Reflect on Your Progress:** Take time to reflect on what worked well and what needs improvement in your time management strategies.

- **Learn to Say No Gracefully:** Practice assertiveness and develop a polite way to decline requests that don't align with your priorities.

- **Set Realistic Goals:** Break down large goals into smaller, achievable tasks to avoid feeling overwhelmed.

- **Reward Yourself:** Acknowledge your progress and celebrate your accomplishments to maintain motivation.

Reclaiming your time and focusing on high-impact activities isn't about working harder; it's about working smarter. By implementing these strategies and cultivating habits of focus, you can unlock your true potential and achieve more with less time. Remember, your time is valuable. Invest it wisely in the activities that truly matter and watch your productivity soar!

Sharpening Your Saw: Expanding Your Skillset Through Collaboration

In today's dynamic job market, continuous learning is crucial for career advancement and success. But what if you don't have to go it alone? This guide explores the power of **leveraging other professionals' expertise** to **expand your skillset**, equipping you with strategies to learn from your colleagues and peers, and fostering a collaborative learning environment.

Beyond Solo Learning: The Benefits of Collaboration

Learning from others offers a multitude of benefits that traditional solo learning might lack:

- **Exposure to Diverse Perspectives:** Collaboration exposes you to different approaches and viewpoints, enriching your understanding and sparking innovation.

- **Accelerated Learning:** Learning from experienced professionals can fast-track your skill development by providing shortcuts and practical insights.

- **Enhanced Problem-Solving:** Collaboration fosters brainstorming and knowledge sharing, leading to more creative and effective solutions.

- **Improved Communication:** Working with others hones your communication skills as you explain concepts, ask questions, and provide feedback.

- **Building Relationships:** Collaboration strengthens relationships with colleagues, fostering a culture of mutual support and learning.

Identifying Learning Opportunities:

There's a wealth of expertise readily available within your professional network. Here's how to identify learning opportunities:

- **Seek Mentorship:** Identify experienced colleagues who possess the skills you wish to develop. Approach them for mentorship opportunities.

- **Initiate Knowledge-Sharing Sessions:** Organize informal sessions where colleagues can share their expertise on specific topics.

- **Participate in Cross-Functional Teams:** Volunteer for projects that involve collaborating with professionals from different departments, exposing you to new skillsets.

- **Observe and Learn:** Pay close attention to how skilled colleagues approach their work. Ask questions and actively seek their insights.

- **Engage in Peer Learning:** Form study groups or learning circles with colleagues to share resources, discuss challenges, and hold each other accountable.

Strategies for Effective Collaboration Learning:

Here's your toolkit to maximize your learning experience through collaborative efforts:

- **Set Clear Learning Goals:** Before seeking collaboration, define your specific learning objectives to guide your interactions.

- **Be an Active Listener:** Pay close attention to your colleagues' insights and ask clarifying questions to gain a deeper understanding.

- **Offer Value in Return:** Collaboration is a two-way street. Offer your own expertise in exchange for learning from others.

- **Practice Respectful Communication:** Maintain a respectful and open-minded approach throughout collaborative learning experiences.

- **Express Gratitude:** Thank your colleagues for their time and willingness to share their expertise.

Building a Collaborative Learning Culture:

Fostering a collaborative learning environment benefits everyone. Here are some ways to make it happen:

- **Champion Knowledge Sharing:** Encourage open communication and knowledge sharing within your team or organization.

- **Organize Learning Sessions:** Organize workshops, seminars, or brown bag lunches for colleagues to share their knowledge.

- **Promote Mentorship Programs:** Actively promote mentorship programs within your organization to connect experienced professionals with those seeking guidance.

- **Create Knowledge-Sharing Platforms:** Utilize internal wikis, forums, or communication channels dedicated to sharing knowledge and resources.

- **Recognize Collaborative Learning:** Acknowledge and reward colleagues who actively participate in knowledge sharing and collaborative learning initiatives.

Leveraging other professionals' expertise is a powerful strategy for expanding your skillset and accelerating your professional growth. By embracing collaboration, seeking opportunities to learn from colleagues, and fostering a culture of knowledge sharing, you can continuously develop your skillset and remain competitive in the ever-evolving job market. Remember, learning is a lifelong journey. Embrace collaboration, and watch your expertise and career prospects flourish!

Consider Virtual Assistants, Freelancers, or Online Tools

Stretch Your Dollar: Finding Affordable Solutions that Suit Your Budget and Needs

Financial well-being hinges on smart spending. But in today's world, it can be easy to feel like everything comes at a premium. This guide equips you with powerful strategies to **find affordable solutions** that meet your needs without breaking the bank.

The Challenge of Affordability:

Finding affordable solutions goes beyond simply looking for the cheapest option. Here's why:

- **Balancing Quality and Cost:** The cheapest option might not be the best quality, leading to frequent replacements or repairs, negating any initial savings.

- **Hidden Costs:** Beware of hidden fees, subscriptions, or maintenance costs associated with seemingly "affordable" options.

- **Prioritizing Needs vs. Wants:** It's crucial to differentiate between needs – essential items – and wants – desirable but non-essential items.

Developing a Budgeting Mindset:

Before seeking affordable solutions, establish a solid understanding of your finances:

- **Track Your Income and Expenses:** Gain a clear picture of your incoming and outgoing funds. Utilize budgeting apps or spreadsheets to categorize your spending.

- **Set Financial Goals:** Define your short-term and long-term financial goals, like saving for a down payment or a dream vacation.

- **Prioritize Needs Over Wants:** Distinguish between essential expenses and impulse purchases. Allocate your resources towards your needs first.

Strategies for Finding Affordable Solutions:

Here's your arsenal of tactics to unearth budget-friendly options:

- **Embrace Comparison Shopping:** Don't settle for the first price you see. Compare prices across different retailers, online marketplaces, and discount stores.

- **Consider Used Alternatives:** Explore pre-owned items in good condition for significant savings. Consider online marketplaces, consignment shops, or garage sales.

- **Utilize Discount Programs:** Take advantage of student discounts, senior citizen discounts, or loyalty programs to reduce costs.

- **Negotiate When Possible:** Don't be afraid to negotiate, especially for services or larger purchases.

- **Explore Free Resources:** Many libraries offer free books, movies, and even online courses. Utilize community resources like parks, recreation centers, or free cultural events.

- **DIY (Do-It-Yourself):** Consider learning basic repairs or maintenance tasks to save on professional service costs. There are countless online tutorials and resources available.

- **Borrow Instead of Buy:** For infrequently used items, consider borrowing from friends, family, or libraries instead of purchasing them.

Planning and Long-Term Savings:

Planning and strategic thinking can unlock even greater affordability:

- **Invest in Quality:** While upfront costs might be higher, investing in quality items that last longer can save you money in the long run.

- **Plan for Maintenance:** Factor in potential maintenance costs when evaluating the affordability of an item.

- **Embrace Preventative Care:** Regular maintenance of electronics, appliances, or vehicles can prevent costly breakdowns later.

- **Utilize Public Transportation or Carpooling:** Reduce transportation costs by utilizing public transportation systems, carpooling with colleagues, or cycling/walking when feasible.

- **Cook at Home:** Eating out frequently can significantly impact your budget. Plan and prepare meals at home for a more affordable and often healthier option.

Building Habits for Financial Savvy:

Financial well-being is an ongoing process. Here are some habits to cultivate a culture of mindful spending:

- **Review Your Budget Regularly:** Revisit and adjust your budget periodically as your needs and income levels evolve.

- **Track Your Progress:** Monitor your spending and celebrate your progress towards achieving your financial goals.

- **Resist Impulse Purchases:** Develop a system to avoid impulse purchases. Implement a "waiting period" before buying non-essential items.

- **Embrace Frugal Living:** Explore ways to reduce your overall spending without compromising your quality of life. Consider free or low-cost entertainment options.

- **Seek Support:** Don't be afraid to seek guidance from financial advisors or budgeting experts for personalized advice.

Finding affordable solutions isn't about deprivation; it's about making smart choices. By embracing these strategies, developing a budget-conscious mindset, and cultivating habits of mindful spending, you can stretch your dollar further and achieve your financial goals. Remember, affordability doesn't mean sacrificing quality of life. It's about finding the balance between your needs and your budget, empowering you to live well within your means.

Bridging the Gap: Ensuring Clear Communication and Quality Control

In any successful endeavor, clear communication and quality control are the cornerstones of achievement. **Clear communication** ensures everyone is on the same page, working towards a shared vision. **Quality control** safeguards the integrity of the work, minimizing errors and ensuring a final product or service that meets expectations. This guide explores the importance of both and equips you with strategies to **bridge the gap** between them, fostering a collaborative environment that delivers exceptional results.

The Importance of Clear Communication:

Clear communication goes beyond simply exchanging information. It's about creating a space for understanding, transparency, and shared goals. Here's why it matters:

- **Reduced Errors and Misunderstandings:** Clear communication minimizes confusion and misinterpretations, leading to fewer errors and rework.

- **Enhanced Collaboration:** Open communication fosters collaboration by ensuring everyone is aware of their roles, responsibilities, and expectations.

- **Improved Problem-Solving:** Effective communication allows for a free flow of ideas and facilitates better problem-solving as a team.

- **Increased Efficiency:** Reduced misunderstandings and a clear understanding of goals lead to more efficient use of time and resources.

- **Boosted Morale:** When everyone feels heard and understood, morale improves, fostering a more positive and productive work environment.

The Importance of Quality Control:

Quality control safeguards the final product or service, ensuring it meets established standards. Here's why it matters:

- **Reduced Costs:** Identifying and correcting errors early in the process prevents costly rework and ensures a high-quality final product.

- **Enhanced Customer Satisfaction:** Delivering consistent quality builds trust and satisfaction with your product or service.

- **Maintained Reputation:** A commitment to quality control protects your brand reputation and fosters customer loyalty.

- **Improved Innovation:** The quality control process can identify areas for improvement, leading to new ideas and innovations.

- **Increased Efficiency:** By catching errors early, you streamline your workflow and reduce wasted time and resources.

The Synergy Between Communication and Quality Control:

Clear communication and quality control are not separate entities; they work hand-in-hand. Here's how they connect:

- **Communicating Requirements:** Clearly defined project requirements and quality standards set the foundation for a successful outcome.

- **Providing Feedback:** Open communication allows for timely and constructive feedback throughout the process, ensuring quality is maintained.

- **Resolving Issues:** Effective communication facilitates the identification and resolution of quality control issues before they escalate.

- **Documentation and Transparency:** Clear documentation of processes, procedures, and quality control standards ensures everyone is on the same page.

- **Celebrating Success:** Communicating successes and improvements in quality control motivates teams and reinforces a culture of excellence.

Strategies for Bridging the Gap:

Here's your toolkit to create a seamless connection between communication and quality control:

- Establish Clear Communication Channels: Define clear channels for communication between team members, clients, and stakeholders.

- Document Everything: Document project requirements, quality control procedures, and communication logs to ensure clarity and consistency.

- Regularly Review Communication: Schedule regular meetings or check-ins to discuss project progress, address any communication gaps, and ensure everyone is aligned.

- Implement Feedback Mechanisms: Establish clear and accessible channels for providing and receiving feedback throughout the project lifecycle.

- Embrace Transparency: Promote transparency by sharing information openly and proactively addressing any potential issues or challenges.

Technology as a Bridge:

Technology can be a powerful tool for fostering clear communication and quality control:

- **Project Management Tools:** Utilize project management platforms for task tracking, communication, and document sharing.

- **Quality Control Software:** Explore software solutions designed to automate and streamline quality control processes.

- **Communication Platforms:** Utilize instant messaging platforms or video conferencing tools to facilitate real-time communication and collaboration.

- **Feedback and Review Tools:** Implement online platforms for receiving and managing feedback on projects and deliverables.

Building a Culture of Excellence:

Both communication and quality control require ongoing effort. Here are some habits to cultivate a culture of excellence:

- **Lead by Example:** Leaders who prioritize clear communication and a commitment to quality set the tone for the entire team.

- **Invest in Training:** Provide training on effective communication skills and quality control procedures for all team members.

- **Empower Employees:** Empower employees to take ownership of their work and to communicate any concerns regarding quality control.

- **Celebrate Achievements:** Acknowledge and celebrate successes in communication and quality control to reinforce the importance of both.

- **Continuously Improve:** Regularly review your communication and quality control processes and seek opportunities for improvement.

Clear communication and quality control are the bedrock of success in any field. By implementing these strategies and fostering a culture of open communication and continuous improvement, you can ensure that everyone is aligned, quality is maintained, and your projects reach their full potential. Remember, clear communication bridges the gap between intention and execution, while quality control safeguards the integrity of your work. Embrace both, and watch your endeavors flourish!

Create a Dedicated Workspace (and Keep it Organized)

Designate a Specific Area for Focused Work

Conquering the Scatterbrain: Minimizing Distractions and Encouraging a Productive Mindset

In our increasingly digital world, distractions lurk around every corner – from social media notifications to the allure of that second (or tenth) browser tab. Maintaining focus and cultivating a productive mindset can feel like an uphill battle. But fear not! This guide equips you with powerful strategies to **minimize distractions** and **encourage a productive mindset**, empowering you to achieve more with less mental clutter.

The Toll of Distraction:

Distractions don't just disrupt our workflow; they have a significant impact on our productivity and well-being:

- **Reduced Focus:** Constant interruptions hinder our ability to concentrate deeply and deliver our best work.

- **Increased Stress:** The feeling of being constantly bombarded with stimuli can lead to chronic stress and anxiety.

- **Decision Fatigue:** Making numerous micro-decisions about responding to distractions can deplete our mental resources.

- **Wasted Time:** The cumulative effect of even small distractions can significantly eat away at valuable time.

- **Decreased Motivation:** The constant struggle to maintain focus can lead to feelings of frustration and hinder motivation.

Identifying Your Distraction Triggers:

The first step to minimizing distractions is understanding what pulls you away from your work:

- **Digital Distractions:** Social media notifications, email alerts, and browser tabs can be major focus disruptors.

- **Physical Environment:** Clutter, uncomfortable workspace, or background noise can all contribute to distraction.

- **Internal Distractions:** Worry, hunger, or fatigue can make it difficult to focus on the task at hand.

- **Multitasking:** Contrary to popular belief, multitasking hinders efficiency and increases mental strain.

Strategies for Minimizing Distractions:

Here's your arsenal of techniques to silence the noise and reclaim your focus:

- **Silence Notifications:** Turn off notifications for social media, email, and other distracting apps during work hours.

- **Utilize Focus Tools:** Explore browser extensions or apps that block distracting websites for a set period of time.

- **Create a Dedicated Workspace:** Designate a specific area for work, free from clutter and conducive to focus.

- **Schedule Time for Distractions:** Allocate specific times in your schedule to check email, social media, or make personal calls.

- **Embrace the Power of "Do Not Disturb":** Inform colleagues and clients about dedicated work hours and utilize "Do Not Disturb" features when needed.

- **Practice Mindfulness:** Engage in mindfulness exercises like meditation or deep breathing to clear your mind and refocus.

Cultivating a Productive Mindset:

Beyond minimizing distractions, fostering a productive mindset is key to achieving your goals:

- **Set Clear Goals:** Having a clear understanding of your goals and objectives provides direction and motivation.

- **Prioritize Ruthlessly:** Identify the most important tasks (high-impact activities) and focus your energy on those first.

- **Break Down Large Tasks:** Divide large projects into smaller, more manageable chunks to avoid feeling overwhelmed.

- **Reward Yourself:** Acknowledge your progress and celebrate your accomplishments to maintain motivation.

- **Embrace a Positive Attitude:** A positive outlook fosters resilience and helps you bounce back from setbacks.

- **Get Enough Sleep:** Prioritize quality sleep; a well-rested mind is better equipped to focus and perform at its best.

Building Habits for Laser Focus:

Maintaining a productive mindset is an ongoing process. Here are some habits to cultivate a culture of focus and achievement:

- **Schedule Focused Work Sessions:** Block dedicated time slots in your calendar for focused work and treat these times as sacred.

- **Practice the Pomodoro Technique:** Utilize the Pomodoro Technique – work in focused 25-minute intervals with short breaks in between – to maintain focus and prevent burnout.

- **Review Your Progress Regularly:** Periodically review your progress, assess what's working well, and identify areas for improvement in your focus strategies.

- **Minimize Multitasking:** Train yourself to focus on one task at a time and avoid switching between tasks constantly.

- **Learn to Say No:** Politely decline requests that don't align with your priorities or would disrupt your focus during dedicated work time.

Minimizing distractions and cultivating a productive mindset are not magic tricks; they require intentionality and practice. By implementing these strategies, building habits of focus, and creating a supportive environment, you can silence the distractions and unlock your full potential. Remember, you are in control of your attention. Take charge, minimize distractions, and watch your productivity soar!

Striking the Right Balance: Separating Work and Personal Life for a Fulfilling Life

In today's constantly connected world, achieving a healthy work-life balance can feel like a constant tightrope walk. Work bleeds into personal time, and personal obligations intrude on professional commitments. But fear not! This guide explores the importance of **separating work and personal life** and equips you with powerful strategies to create boundaries, foster well-being, and achieve a more fulfilling life.

Why Separate Work and Personal Life?

Maintaining a clear separation between work and personal life isn't about segregation; it's about intentionality and well-being. Here's why it matters:

- **Reduced Stress and Burnout:** Constant connectivity can lead to chronic stress and burnout. Boundaries allow for relaxation and rejuvenation.

- **Improved Focus and Productivity:** A clear separation allows you to be fully present and focused during work hours, leading to better results.

- **Enhanced Personal Relationships:** Dedicating time and energy to loved ones strengthens relationships and fosters a sense of connection outside of work.

- **Increased Overall Well-being:** A healthy work-life balance promotes physical, mental, and emotional well-being, leading to a more fulfilling life.

- **Prevention of Resentment:** Boundaries help prevent feelings of resentment from building up due to work-life imbalance.

Challenges of Separation:

Achieving a healthy separation comes with its own set of challenges:

- **The "Always On" Culture:** Technology and constant connectivity blur the lines between work and personal time.

- **Demanding Workloads:** Heavy workloads and tight deadlines can make it difficult to "switch off" after work.

- **Fear of Missing Out (FOMO):** The pressure to be constantly available can make it hard to disconnect from work.

- **Unrealistic Expectations:** Both personal and professional expectations can make it difficult to achieve a perfect balance.

Strategies for Effective Separation:

Here's your toolkit to create healthy boundaries and achieve a more balanced life:

- **Set Clear Work Hours:** Define specific work hours and stick to them as much as possible. Communicate these boundaries to colleagues and clients.

- **Utilize Time Management Techniques:** Employ effective time management strategies to maximize productivity during work hours and minimize the need to work outside of them.

- **Power Down After Work:** Resist the urge to check work emails or messages outside of work hours. Turn off work notifications and silence work devices.

- **Schedule Personal Time:** Block out time in your calendar for personal activities, hobbies, and spending time with loved ones. Treat this time as important as work commitments.

- **Create a Dedicated Workspace:** Designate a specific area for work, and avoid working from your bed or relaxation zones. This helps signal a shift between work mode and personal mode.

- **Communicate Boundaries:** Openly communicate your boundaries to colleagues, managers, and family members. Explain your need for dedicated personal time.

- **Embrace the Power of "No":** Learn to politely decline requests that would disrupt your personal time or work outside of your designated work hours.

Technology as a Tool:

Technology can be a double-edged sword. Here's how to use it to your advantage:

- **Utilize Time Management Apps:** Explore apps that help you schedule work time, block distracting websites, and track your progress towards achieving a work-life balance.

- **Silence Notifications:** Utilize features on your devices to silence notifications for work emails and apps outside of work hours.

- **Utilize Out-of-Office Messages:** Set up an out-of-office message during non-working hours to manage expectations and discourage work communication.

- **Explore Focus Tools:** Utilize browser extensions or apps that block distracting websites for a set period of time, allowing you to focus on personal activities.

Building Habits for a Balanced Life:

Creating a healthy work-life balance is an ongoing process. Here are some habits to cultivate a sustainable approach:

- **Regularly Review Your Schedule:** Periodically assess your work-life balance and adjust your schedule or boundaries as needed.

- **Practice Mindfulness:** Engage in mindfulness exercises like meditation or deep breathing to manage stress and improve your ability to disconnect from work.

- **Prioritize Self-Care:** Schedule time for activities that promote your physical and mental well-being, such as exercise, hobbies, or spending time in nature.

- **Lead by Example:** If you are a manager, set boundaries yourself and encourage your team members to do the same.

- **Seek Support:** Don't be afraid to seek support from friends, family, or a therapist if you struggle to achieve a healthy work-life balance.

Creating a healthy separation between work and personal life is an investment in your well-being, your productivity, and the quality of your relationships. By establishing boundaries, managing your time effectively, and prioritizing both work and personal time, you can achieve a work-life balance that fosters happiness, success, and a fulfilling life. Remember, disconnection from work isn't a sign of weakness; it's a necessity for a thriving and sustainable career and personal life.

Maintain a Clutter-Free Environment with Organizational Systems

Clear the Clutter, Boost Your Bottom Line: Effective Storage Solutions and Decluttering Strategies

Disorganization can be a silent productivity drain. A cluttered workspace or overloaded digital storage can hinder your ability to focus, find information quickly, and ultimately, limit your earning potential. This guide equips you with powerful **storage solutions** and **decluttering strategies**, empowering you to transform your physical and digital space, unlock improved productivity, and increase your income potential.

The Cost of Clutter:

Clutter goes beyond just misplaced items. It can have a significant impact on your well-being and financial success:

Reduced Productivity: Time wasted searching for lost items or information hinders efficiency and income generation.

Increased Stress: Visual clutter and a disorganized environment can contribute to chronic stress and anxiety.

Hindered Creativity: A cluttered space can stifle creative thinking and problem-solving abilities.

Missed Opportunities: Disorganized finances or misplaced paperwork can lead to missed deadlines or lost opportunities.

Negative Perception: A cluttered workspace can create a negative impression on clients or colleagues.

The Power of Organization:

Effective storage solutions and decluttering strategies offer a multitude of benefits:

Enhanced Focus: A clean and organized environment minimizes distractions and allows you to focus on the task at hand.

Improved Efficiency: Easy access to information and essential items saves valuable time and boosts productivity.

Reduced Stress: A clutter-free space fosters a sense of calm and reduces stress levels.

Increased Creativity: An organized environment allows for clearer thinking and can spark new ideas.

Boosted Confidence: A well-organized workspace can project a professional image and boost your confidence.

Effective Storage Solutions:

Here's your arsenal of tools to tame the clutter and create a more functional space:

Utilize Storage Containers: Employ labeled containers, shelves, and drawers to categorize and organize items in your workspace and home office.

Embrace Vertical Space: Utilize wall shelves, cabinets, or hanging organizers to maximize storage capacity without sacrificing floor space.

Implement a Filing System: Develop a clear and consistent filing system for physical and digital documents to ensure easy retrieval.

Invest in Multi-Functional Furniture: Explore furniture with built-in storage compartments to maximize space utilization.

Utilize Cloud Storage Solutions: Consider cloud storage solutions for digital documents and files, ensuring accessibility from any device.

Decluttering Strategies for Success:

Here's your action plan to transform your space and unlock its full potential:

The One-Touch Rule: When handling an item, decide to keep it, toss it, or relocate it immediately. Avoid the "maybe" pile.

Start Small: Don't get overwhelmed. Begin by decluttering a single drawer, shelf, or digital folder at a time.

Embrace the Power of "No": Learn to politely decline free items that you don't truly need or won't use.

Utilize the "KonMari" Method: This method encourages keeping items that "spark joy" and discarding those that don't.

Schedule Regular Decluttering Sessions: Integrate decluttering into your routine to prevent clutter from accumulating again.

The Link Between Organization and Income:

Effective storage solutions and decluttering strategies can indirectly boost your income potential:

Increased Productivity: Improved efficiency translates to more work completed in less time, leading to higher earning potential.

Reduced Time Waste: Minimized time spent searching for lost items or information frees up valuable time for income-generating activities.

Enhanced Client Perception: A well-organized workspace creates a professional image, fostering client trust and potentially leading to more business opportunities.

Improved Sales and Marketing Materials: Organized digital files ensure access to high-quality marketing materials, impacting sales efforts.

Better Financial Management: Organized financial documents streamline tax filing, budgeting, and overall financial well-being, potentially saving money.

Building Habits for Lasting Order:

Maintaining an organized space requires ongoing effort. Here are some habits to cultivate a culture of order:

Put Things Away Immediately: Develop the habit of returning items to their designated storage space after each use.

Declutter Regularly: Schedule regular decluttering sessions to prevent clutter from accumulating again.

Resist Impulse Purchases: Be mindful of your purchases and avoid acquiring items you don't truly need.

Embrace Minimalism: Consider adopting a minimalist mindset, focusing on keeping only what you truly use and value.

Lead by Example: If you have a team, encourage them to adopt organizational practices as well.

Decluttering and implementing effective storage solutions aren't just about creating a neater space;

they're about creating an environment that empowers you to thrive. By embracing these strategies, you can boost your productivity, unlock income potential, and experience the joy of a calm and organized space. Remember, a little effort can go a long way in improving productivity and income.

Sharpen Your Focus, Boost Your Bottom Line: Promoting Clarity and Reducing Time Wasted Searching

In today's fast-paced world, **clarity is king**. Knowing exactly what you need, when you need it, is fundamental for peak productivity and maximizing your income potential. Time spent searching for tools, materials, or information is time wasted, hindering progress and impacting your bottom line. This guide equips you with powerful strategies to **promote clarity** and **reduce wasted search time**, empowering you to work smarter, not harder, and achieve more in less time.

The Cost of Confusion:

A lack of clarity has a ripple effect, impacting your productivity and income:

Wasted Time: Searching for lost items, misplaced tools, or forgotten information eats away at valuable work time.

Reduced Efficiency: Confusion and indecision hinder your ability to make quick and confident decisions.

Increased Stress: The frustration of not knowing where things are or what to do next contributes to chronic stress.

Missed Deadlines: Delays caused by searching can lead to missed deadlines and potential lost income.

Lower Quality Work: The inability to focus due to confusion can lead to rushed or error-prone work.

The Power of Clarity:

Promoting clarity offers a multitude of benefits:

Enhanced Focus: A clear understanding of tasks and goals allows you to focus your energy on what truly matters.

Improved Decision-Making: Clarity empowers you to make quick and confident decisions based on all the available information.

Reduced Stress: Knowing what to do next and where things are minimizes frustration and promotes a sense of calm.

Increased Productivity: Reduced search time translates to more time spent on income-generating activities.

Improved Quality of Work: Clear focus allows you to produce higher-quality work with fewer errors.

Strategies for Promoting Clarity:

Here's your toolkit to banish confusion and embrace a focused workflow:

Clearly Define Goals and Objectives: Before starting any project, clearly define your goals and objectives. This provides a roadmap for your actions.

Develop Detailed Plans: Create detailed plans that outline the tasks required, resources needed, and timelines for completion.

Utilize Checklists and To-Do Lists: Utilize checklists and to-do lists to break down projects into manageable tasks and track your progress.

Communicate Effectively: Maintain clear and open communication with colleagues, clients, and team members to avoid misunderstandings.

Establish Consistent Organization Systems: Implement consistent organization systems for physical and digital tools, materials, and documents.

Utilize Labeling and Categorization: Clearly label files, folders, tools, and storage containers for easy identification and retrieval.

Embrace Visual Tools: Utilize mind maps, flowcharts, or whiteboards to visualize projects and workflows, promoting clarity.

Reducing Time Wasted Searching:

Here are your tactics to minimize wasted search time and maximize efficiency:

Invest in a Centralized Storage System: Create a centralized storage system for physical and digital resources, ensuring easy access from any location.

Utilize Search Features: Master the search functionalities of your project management tools, file systems, and online resources.

Document Everything: Develop a habit of documenting processes, procedures, and locations of key resources for future reference.

Conduct Regular Audits: Schedule regular audits of your physical and digital workspace to identify and eliminate unnecessary clutter.

Utilize Search Engines and Online Resources: Master the art of using online search engines and industry-specific resources to locate information quickly.

Embrace Technology Solutions: Explore technology solutions like document management systems or asset tracking apps to streamline resource management.

The Link Between Clarity and Increased Income:

Promoting clarity and reducing search time directly impacts your income potential:

More Time for Income-Generating Activities: Reduced search time frees up valuable hours for client work, sales efforts, or other income-generating activities.

Improved Client Satisfaction: Reduced delays and clear communication fosters client satisfaction, potentially leading to repeat business.

Reduced Expenses: Minimizing lost or misplaced tools and materials translates to cost savings.

Enhanced Innovation: Clarity fosters creative thinking and problem-solving, leading to new ideas and potentially increased income streams.

Building Habits for Lasting Clarity:

Maintaining clarity requires ongoing effort. Here are some habits to cultivate a culture of clear communication and efficient workflows:

Schedule Time for Planning: Allocate dedicated time at the beginning of projects for planning, goal setting, and outlining processes.

Embrace Continuous Improvement: Regularly review your processes and communication strategies, and seek opportunities for improvement.

Promote Open Communication: Encourage an environment where team members feel comfortable asking questions and requesting clarification.

Lead by Example: As a leader, demonstrate a commitment to clear communication and well-defined processes.

Invest in Training: Provide training for your team on effective project management, resource management, and communication skills.

Promoting clarity and reducing search time isn't a one-time fix; it's an ongoing process. By implementing these strategies, building habits of clear communication, and fostering a culture of organization, you can transform your projects, minimize wasted time, and unlock significant gains in productivity and income. Remember, clarity is an investment – an investment in your time, your team's well-being, and ultimately, your success.

Cultivate Healthy Habits for Peak Performance

Prioritize Quality Sleep for Improved Focus and Energy

Sleep Well, Earn Well: Establishing a Consistent Sleep Schedule and Prioritizing Rest for Peak Productivity and Income

In our 24/7 world, sleep is often seen as a luxury, not a necessity. But skimping on shut-eye has a significant impact on more than just your mood. It can significantly hinder your productivity and ultimately, your income potential. This guide explores the importance of establishing a **consistent sleep schedule** and **prioritizing rest**, equipping you with strategies to optimize your sleep for peak performance and financial success.

The High Cost of Sleep Deprivation:

Chronic sleep deprivation isn't just about feeling tired. It has a multitude of negative consequences:

- **Reduced Cognitive Function:** Sleep deprivation impairs memory, focus, and decision-making, leading to errors and inefficiencies.

- **Decreased Creativity:** A well-rested mind is more creative and innovative. Sleep deprivation hinders your ability to think outside the box.

- **Lowered Energy Levels:** Feeling constantly fatigued impacts your ability to work long hours and complete tasks efficiently.

- **Increased Stress and Anxiety:** Lack of sleep contributes to chronic stress and anxiety, hindering performance and well-being.

- **Weakened Immune System:** Sleep deprivation weakens your immune system, making you more susceptible to illnesses that can further disrupt your work.

The Power of Quality Sleep:

Prioritizing quality sleep offers a multitude of benefits:

- **Enhanced Cognitive Function:** A well-rested brain is sharper, more focused, and retains information better.

- **Improved Decision-Making:** Quality sleep allows for clearer thinking and better decision-making abilities.

- **Boosted Creativity:** Sleep allows your brain to process information and make connections, fostering creativity and innovation.

- **Increased Energy Levels:** Adequate sleep fuels your body and mind, allowing you to tackle tasks with more energy and stamina.

- **Reduced Stress and Anxiety:** Quality sleep improves your ability to manage stress and anxiety, promoting emotional well-being.

- **Enhanced Physical Health:** Sleep is essential for physical health, promoting tissue repair and overall well-being.

Establishing a Consistent Sleep Schedule:

The key to reaping the benefits of sleep lies in consistency:

- **Identify Your Sleep Needs:** Most adults require 7-8 hours of sleep per night. Listen to your body and determine your optimal sleep duration.

- **Set a Regular Sleep Schedule:** Go to bed and wake up at the same time each day, even on weekends. This regulates your body's natural sleep-wake cycle.

- **Create a Relaxing Bedtime Routine:** Develop a calming bedtime routine that signals to your body it's time to wind down. This could include taking a warm bath, reading a book, or practicing relaxation techniques like deep breathing or meditation.

- **Optimize Your Sleep Environment:** Ensure your bedroom is dark, quiet, cool, and clutter-free to promote restful sleep.

- **Limit Screen Time Before Bed:** The blue light emitted from electronic devices disrupts sleep patterns. Avoid screens for at least an hour before bedtime.

- **Develop a Power Down Ritual:** Power down electronic devices at least an hour before bed and avoid using them in bed.

- **Regular Exercise:** Regular physical activity promotes better sleep, but avoid strenuous workouts close to bedtime.

- **Manage Stress:** Chronic stress can significantly disrupt sleep. Develop healthy coping mechanisms to manage stress levels.

- **Limit Caffeine and Alcohol:** Minimize caffeine intake, especially in the afternoon and evening, as it can interfere with sleep. Avoid excessive alcohol consumption, which disrupts sleep patterns.

Prioritizing Rest Beyond Sleep:

Quality sleep is just one piece of the rest equation:

- **Schedule Breaks Throughout the Day:** Take short breaks throughout the workday to get up, move around, and refresh your mind.

- **Schedule Time for Relaxation:** Integrate activities like meditation, yoga, or spending time in nature into your routine to promote relaxation and reduce stress.

- **Learn to Say No:** Don't overload your schedule. Learn to politely decline requests that would compromise your sleep or rest time.

- **Delegate When Possible:** Delegate tasks whenever possible to avoid burnout and ensure you have sufficient time for rest.

- **Take Vacations:** Regular vacations provide much-needed mental and physical breaks, leading to increased productivity upon return.

The Link Between Sleep and Increased Income:

Prioritizing sleep and rest directly impacts your earning potential:

- **Improved Efficiency:** A well-rested mind works faster and more efficiently, leading to increased output and a higher quality of work.

- **Reduced Errors:** Sleep deprivation increases the likelihood of errors, which can cost time and money to rectify.

- **Enhanced Creativity:** Quality sleep fosters creativity, potentially leading to new ideas and innovations that can boost your income.

- **Improved Client Satisfaction:** Better focus and communication skills lead to improved client satisfaction and potentially repeat business.

Reduced Absenteeism: Adequate sleep strengthens your immune system that translates to fewer sick days and a more reliable presence at work.

- **Improved Memory and Recall:** Sleep strengthens memory consolidation and recall, allowing you to retain important information.

Breaking the Cycle: Avoiding Late-Night Work Sessions for Peak Productivity and Income

The allure of the "all-nighter" can be strong, especially when deadlines loom. But those late-night work sessions often come at a cost. Burning the midnight oil can significantly **impact your productivity** and, ultimately, your **income**. This guide equips you with powerful strategies to **avoid late-night work sessions** and embrace a sustainable work schedule that fosters peak performance and financial success.

The Pitfalls of Late-Night Work:

While a late-night session might seem productive in the short term, the long-term consequences are significant:

- **Decreased Cognitive Function:** Sleep deprivation impairs focus, memory, and decision-making, leading to errors and inefficiencies the next day.

- **Reduced Creativity:** A well-rested mind is more creative. Late nights hinder new ideas and problem-solving abilities.

- **Increased Stress and Anxiety:** The pressure to complete tasks coupled with sleep deprivation fuels stress and anxiety, impacting well-being.

- **Lowered Energy Levels:** Feeling fatigued throughout the day hinders productivity and motivation.

- **Weakened Immune System:** Chronic sleep deprivation weakens your immune system, making you more susceptible to illnesses that can further disrupt your workflow.

The Benefits of a Defined Work Schedule:

Establishing a clear work schedule offers a multitude of benefits:

- **Improved Sleep Quality:** A regular sleep schedule promotes deeper and more restful sleep, leading to increased energy levels the next day.

- **Enhanced Focus and Clarity:** A well-rested mind is sharper and can maintain focus for longer periods, leading to better decision-making.

- **Boosted Creativity and Problem-Solving:** A fresh mind fosters creativity and innovation, leading to better solutions and new ideas.

- **Improved Work-Life Balance:** A defined schedule allows for dedicated time for personal life and activities outside of work, promoting well-being.

- **Reduced Stress and Burnout:** Sticking to a work schedule helps manage stress levels and prevents burnout.

Strategies for Avoiding Late Nights:

Here's your toolkit to reclaim your evenings and work smarter, not later:

- **Prioritize ruthlessly:** Identify the most important tasks (high-impact activities) and focus on those during your core work hours.

- **Utilize Time Management Techniques:** Employ effective time management strategies like the Eisenhower Matrix or the Pomodoro Technique to maximize productivity during your designated work time.

- **Set Realistic Deadlines:** Avoid setting unrealistic deadlines that push you towards late nights.

- **Communicate Effectively:** Communicate potential delays or workload challenges proactively with clients or colleagues.

- **Delegate When Possible:** Don't be afraid to delegate tasks when possible to avoid work overload and the need for late-night sessions.

- **Learn to Say No:** Don't overload your schedule. Politely decline new work requests if they would force you to work late.

- **Schedule "Power Down" Time:** Block out time in your calendar to unwind and disconnect from work in the evenings.

- **Schedule Breaks Throughout the Day:** Take short breaks throughout the workday to get up, move around, and refresh your mind.

- **Develop a Relaxing Pre-Sleep Routine:** Create a calming bedtime routine that signals to your body it's time to wind down and prepare for sleep.

- **Optimize Your Sleep Environment:** Ensure your bedroom is dark, quiet, cool, and clutter-free for a more restful night's sleep.

Building Habits for Sustainable Success:

Avoiding late-night work sessions requires ongoing effort:

- **Track Your Time:** Monitor your work hours to identify areas for improvement and ensure you're utilizing your time efficiently during the day.

- **Review Regularly:** Periodically assess your work schedule and workload to ensure it's sustainable and allows you to maintain a healthy work-life balance.

- **Lead by Example:** If you have a team, establish clear expectations regarding work hours and discourage late-night work sessions.

- **Reward Yourself:** Celebrate your successes in sticking to your schedule and prioritizing your well-being.

- **Seek Support:** If you struggle to disconnect from work in the evenings, seek support from a therapist or life coach to develop healthy coping mechanisms.

The Link Between Early Nights and Increased Income:

By avoiding late-night work sessions, you're investing in your most valuable asset – yourself. Here's how:

- **Enhanced Productivity:** A well-rested mind is more productive, leading to a higher quality of work and potentially increased earning potential.

- **Improved Decision-Making:** Better focus and clear thinking lead to better decision-making, potentially leading to fewer costly mistakes.

- **Reduced Absenteeism:** Adequate sleep strengthens your immune system, leading to fewer sick days and increased work time.

- **Enhanced Creativity:** A well-rested mind fosters creative thinking, potentially leading to new ideas and innovations that can boost your income.

- **Reduced Errors:** Fatigue-induced errors require revisions and corrections, wasting valuable time and resources.

Prioritizing sleep, structure, and focus can dramatically improve your productivity and well-being. By **avoiding late-night work sessions**, you can reclaim your time, enhance your work quality, and ultimately **increase your earning potential**.

Eat Nutritious Foods and Stay Hydrated

Fueling Your Success: Maintaining a Healthy Diet for Peak Productivity

You are what you eat. This age-old adage holds immense truth, especially when it comes to **productivity** and **income**. The food you choose not only impacts your physical health but also significantly affects your mental well-being, focus, and ultimately, your earning potential. This guide explores the importance of maintaining a **healthy diet** and equips you with powerful strategies to make informed food choices that fuel your body and mind for peak performance and financial success.

The Cost of Unhealthy Eating:

A diet laden with processed foods, sugary drinks, and unhealthy fats can have a significant negative impact:

- **Reduced Energy Levels:** Unhealthy foods lead to blood sugar spikes and crashes, leaving you feeling sluggish and unfocused throughout the day.

- **Brain Fog and Decreased Cognitive Function:** A diet lacking in essential nutrients can impair focus, memory, and decision-making, hindering productivity.

- **Increased Stress and Anxiety:** Unhealthy eating habits can contribute to chronic stress and anxiety, impacting your emotional well-being.

- **Weakened Immune System:** A poor diet weakens your immune system, making you more susceptible to illnesses that can disrupt your work schedule.

- **Presenteeism with Reduced Efficiency:** Even if you're physically present at work, unhealthy eating can lead to reduced productivity and increased errors.

The Power of a Healthy Diet:

Nourishing your body with the right foods offers a multitude of benefits:

- **Sustained Energy Levels:** A diet rich in complex carbohydrates, lean protein, and healthy fats provides sustained energy throughout the day, promoting peak performance.

- **Enhanced Focus and Clarity:** The right nutrients fuel your brain, leading to improved focus, memory, and cognitive function.

- **Reduced Stress and Improved Mood:** Eating healthy foods can boost your mood and improve your ability to manage stress.

- **Stronger Immune System:** A diet rich in essential vitamins and minerals strengthens your immune system, leading to fewer sick days and increased work time.

- **Improved Overall Well-being:** Nourishing your body with healthy foods promotes physical and mental well-being, allowing you to bring your best self to work.

Essential Components of a Brain-Boosting Diet:

Here's a roadmap to building a diet that fuels your success:

- **Focus on Whole Foods:** Prioritize whole, unprocessed foods like fruits, vegetables, whole grains, lean protein sources, and healthy fats.

- **Stay Hydrated:** Drinking plenty of water is essential for optimal brain function. Aim for eight glasses of water daily.

- **Embrace Fruits and Vegetables:** Fruits and vegetables are packed with essential vitamins, minerals, and antioxidants that support brain health.

- **Choose Lean Protein Sources:** Lean protein sources like fish, chicken, beans, and lentils provide sustained energy and support cognitive function.

- **Include Healthy Fats:** Healthy fats like those found in avocados, nuts, and olive oil are essential for brain health and cognitive function.

- **Limit Processed Foods:** Processed foods are often high in sugar, unhealthy fats, and sodium, which can negatively impact your brain function and energy levels.

- **Reduce Sugar Intake:** Excessive sugar intake can lead to blood sugar crashes and hinder focus.

- **Mind Your Portions:** Practice mindful eating and avoid overeating, which can lead to sluggishness and decreased productivity.

- **Plan and Prep Meals:** Planning and prepping meals in advance helps you make healthy choices and avoid unhealthy temptations when pressed for time.

Building Habits for Long-Term Health:

Maintaining a healthy diet requires ongoing effort:

- **Read Food Labels:** Develop the habit of reading food labels to understand ingredients and make informed choices.

- **Cook More at Home:** Cooking at home allows you to control the ingredients in your meals and ensure you're consuming healthy options.

- **Prepare Healthy Snacks:** Keep healthy snacks like fruits, nuts, or yogurt readily available to avoid unhealthy vending machine choices.

- **Stay Mindful of Emotional Eating:** Identify and address the root cause of emotional eating to avoid unhealthy patterns.

- **Seek Support:** If you struggle to maintain a healthy diet, consider consulting a registered dietitian for personalized guidance.

The Link Between Healthy Eating and Increased Income:

By prioritizing a healthy diet, you're investing in your most valuable asset – yourself. Here's how it translates to increased income:

- **Enhanced Productivity:** A well-nourished brain is more productive, leading to a higher quality of work and potentially increased earning potential.

- **Improved Decision-Making:** Better focus and clear thinking lead to better decision-making, potentially leading to fewer costly mistakes.

- **Reduced Absenteeism:** A strong immune system leads to fewer sick days and increased work time.

- **Increased Confidence and Professionalism:** Taking care of your physical health and well-being can boost your confidence and project a professional image.

- **Enhanced Mood and Resilience:** A healthy diet promotes a positive mood and greater resilience to stress, fostering a better work environment.

Conquering the Afternoon Slump: Avoiding Energy Crashes and Maintaining Focus for Peak Productivity and Income

The afternoon slump is a familiar foe. That mid-day dip in energy and focus can derail your workflow and leave you feeling sluggish. But fear not! Maintaining **consistent energy levels** and **sustained focus** throughout the day is achievable. This guide equips you with powerful strategies to **avoid energy crashes** and **maximize productivity**, ultimately boosting your income potential.

The Culprits Behind Energy Crashes:

Several factors contribute to those dreaded afternoon slumps:

- **Unhealthy Food Choices:** A diet high in processed foods and simple sugars can lead to blood sugar spikes and crashes, leaving you feeling drained.

- **Dehydration:** Not drinking enough water can significantly impact your energy levels and cognitive function.

- **Lack of Sleep:** Chronic sleep deprivation disrupts your body's natural energy cycles, leading to fatigue and difficulty focusing.

- **Sedentary Lifestyle:** A lack of physical activity can contribute to sluggishness and decreased alertness.

- **Stress and Anxiety:** Chronic stress can deplete energy reserves and make it difficult to concentrate.

- **Eye Strain:** Staring at screens for extended periods can lead to eye strain and fatigue.

The Power of Sustained Energy and Focus:

Maintaining consistent energy levels and focus throughout the day offers a multitude of benefits:

- **Enhanced Productivity:** Increased focus and motivation allow you to accomplish more in less time.

- **Improved Decision-Making:** A clear and focused mind leads to better decisions and fewer errors.

- **Reduced Stress and Anxiety:** Sustained energy levels help you manage stress and maintain composure under pressure.

- **Enhanced Creativity:** A well-rested and focused mind fosters creative thinking and problem-solving abilities.

- **Improved Work Quality:** When you're focused, you produce higher-quality work and deliver better results.

Strategies for Staying Energized and Focused:

Here's your action plan to combat afternoon slumps and maintain peak performance throughout the workday:

- **Fuel Your Body with the Right Foods:** Prioritize a healthy diet rich in complex carbohydrates, lean protein, and healthy fats for sustained energy.

- **Hydrate Regularly:** Drink plenty of water throughout the day to stay hydrated and support cognitive function. Aim for eight glasses daily.

- **Prioritize Sleep:** Aim for 7-8 hours of quality sleep each night to recharge your body and mind.

- **Move Your Body:** Schedule regular breaks to get up, move around, and stretch. Consider incorporating short walks or light exercise routines into your workday.

- **Manage Stress:** Develop healthy coping mechanisms for managing stress, such as meditation, deep breathing exercises, or spending time in nature.

- **Minimize Screen Time:** Take breaks from screens to reduce eye strain and refresh your focus.

- **Embrace Natural Light:** Work in areas with natural light whenever possible, as it can boost energy levels and alertness.

- **Utilize the Power of Music:** Upbeat music can elevate mood and improve focus. Experiment with different genres to find what works best for you.

- **Power Down During Breaks:** Avoid checking work emails or messages during breaks. Use this time to truly disconnect and recharge.

- **Schedule Demanding Tasks Strategically:** Identify your peak productivity times and schedule demanding tasks during those periods.

Building Habits for Long-Term Energy:

Maintaining sustained energy and focus requires ongoing effort:

- **Plan Your Meals:** Plan and prepare healthy meals and snacks in advance to avoid unhealthy choices on the go.

- **Set Daily Hydration Goals:** Set reminders to drink water throughout the day and track your progress with a reusable water bottle.

- **Develop a Consistent Sleep Schedule:** Go to bed and wake up at the same time each day, even on weekends, to regulate your sleep-wake cycle.

- **Integrate Movement into Your Routine:** Develop a habit of incorporating short bursts of physical activity into your day, such as taking the stairs or walking during phone calls.

- **Practice Mindfulness Techniques:** Integrate mindfulness practices like meditation or deep breathing into your routine to manage stress and improve focus.

- **Create an Ergonomic Workspace:** Designate a workspace that promotes good posture and minimizes eye strain.

- **Schedule Regular Eye Breaks:** Set reminders to take short breaks from screens every 20-30 minutes to reduce eye strain.

- **Reward Yourself:** Celebrate your successes in maintaining healthy habits and focusing on your well-being.

The Link Between Energy and Increased Income:

By prioritizing sustained energy and focus, you're investing in your most valuable asset – yourself. Here's how it translates to increased income:

- **Increased Productivity:** More work accomplished in less time translates directly to a higher earning potential.

- **Improved Quality of Work:** Better focus leads to higher quality work, potentially leading to increased client satisfaction and repeat business.

- **Reduced Absenteeism:** Maintaining good health minimizes the risk of illnesses and unplanned absences.

Eliminate Distractions and Stay Focused

Silence Notifications and Put Your Phone Away

Silence the Noise, Seize Control: Minimizing Interruptions and Reclaiming Your Time for Peak Productivity and Income

In today's hyper-connected world, distractions and interruptions are constant threats to our productivity and income potential. **Regaining control of your time** and **minimizing interruptions** is crucial for maximizing your focus and achieving your goals. This guide equips you with powerful strategies to **silence the noise**, **reclaim your time**, and work smarter, not harder, to boost your productivity and income.

The Cost of Constant Interruptions:

The constant ping of notifications, unexpected visitors, and multitasking can significantly hinder your performance:

- **Reduced Focus and Concentration:** Interruptions disrupt your thought process and make it challenging to refocus, leading to inefficiencies.

- **Increased Stress and Anxiety:** The constant feeling of being "on" can contribute to chronic stress and anxiety, impacting your well-being and decision-making.

- **Decreased Productivity:** Switching between tasks due to interruptions hinders your ability to complete projects efficiently.

- **Missed Deadlines and Errors:** The inability to focus due to interruptions can lead to missed deadlines and increased errors in your work.

- **Reduced Creativity:** Constant interruptions stifle creativity and innovative thinking, hindering your ability to come up with new ideas.

The Power of Focused Work:

By minimizing interruptions and reclaiming control of your time, you unlock a multitude of benefits:

- **Enhanced Productivity:** Focused work allows you to accomplish more in less time, leading to increased output and a higher quality of work.

- **Improved Decision-Making:** A clear and focused mind fosters better decision-making and problem-solving abilities.

- **Reduced Stress and Anxiety:** Minimizing distractions promotes a calmer and more focused state of mind, leading to reduced stress levels.

- **Enhanced Creativity:** When you can focus on a task without interruptions, your creativity flourishes, allowing you to generate innovative ideas.

- **Greater Job Satisfaction:** Feeling in control of your time and achieving goals leads to increased job satisfaction and motivation.

Strategies for Minimizing Interruptions:

Here's your arsenal of tools to **silence the distractions** and **reclaim your focus**:

- **Communicate Clear Boundaries:** Inform colleagues and clients about your work hours and preferred communication methods.

- **Utilize Time Blocking:** Block out specific time slots in your calendar for focused work on specific tasks.

- **Embrace "Do Not Disturb" Modes:** Utilize "Do Not Disturb" features on phones and email to minimize notifications during focused work sessions.

- **Designate a Quiet Workspace:** If possible, create a dedicated workspace free from distractions like noise and clutter.

- **Manage Notifications Wisely:** Turn off unnecessary notifications on your phone and computer or silence them during focused work periods.

- **Schedule Meetings Strategically:** Group meetings together and avoid scheduling them during peak productivity times.

- **Schedule Email Check-Ins:** Limit yourself to checking emails at specific times throughout the day instead of constantly monitoring your inbox.

- **Delegate When Possible:** Don't be afraid to delegate tasks that can be handled by others, freeing up your time for focused work.

- **Batch Similar Tasks:** Group similar tasks together to minimize context switching and improve efficiency.

- **Learn to Say No:** Don't overload your schedule. Politely decline requests that would significantly disrupt your workflow.

Building Habits for Uninterrupted Focus:

Maintaining focused work requires ongoing effort:

- **Review Your Schedule Regularly:** Periodically assess your work schedule and identify areas where interruptions can be minimized.

- **Lead by Example:** If you have a team, establish clear expectations regarding communication and interruptions.

- **Communicate Proactively:** Inform colleagues and clients when you need uninterrupted time to focus on specific tasks.

- **Reward Yourself:** Celebrate your successes in minimizing interruptions and reclaiming control of your time.

The Link Between Focused Work and Increased Income:

By minimizing interruptions and prioritizing focused work, you're investing in your most valuable asset – yourself. Here's how it translates to increased income:

- **Increased Productivity:** More focused work translates to higher output and potentially increased earning potential.

- **Reduced Errors:** Improved focus leads to fewer errors, saving time and money spent on corrections.

- **Enhanced Client Satisfaction:** Focused work allows you to deliver high-quality work on time, leading to satisfied clients and repeat business.

- **Improved Time Management:** Reclaiming control of your time allows you to prioritize high-impact tasks and projects that contribute most to your income.

- **Reduced Stress and Burnout:** Less stress and a sense of control over your time lead to increased energy and motivation, potentially leading to longer working hours without burnout.

Tech to the Rescue: Utilizing Apps and Settings to Silence Distractions and Boost Your Income

In our digital age, distractions lurk everywhere, from social media notifications to tempting browser tabs. These constant interruptions erode productivity and ultimately, your income potential. But fear not! Technology offers a helping hand. By leveraging **apps and settings** designed to **disable distractions**, you can create a focused work environment and unlock your peak earning potential. This guide equips you with powerful tools and strategies to **silence the digital noise** and **maximize your productivity**.

The Digital Distraction Dilemma:

The constant allure of digital distractions takes a significant toll:

- **Reduced Focus and Concentration:** Notifications and multitasking fragment attention, making it difficult to stay focused on the task at hand.

- **Increased Time Wasted:** Checking emails, social media, or news feeds eats away at valuable work time.

- **Decision Fatigue:** The constant barrage of choices and information leads to decision fatigue, hindering your ability to make sound judgments.

- **Increased Stress and Anxiety:** The feeling of being "on" all the time can contribute to chronic stress and anxiety.

- **Reduced Creativity:** Constant distractions stifle the creative process and innovative thinking.

The Power of a Focused Digital Workspace:

By utilizing apps and settings to minimize digital distractions, you unlock a multitude of benefits:

- **Enhanced Productivity:** Reduced distractions allow you to concentrate on tasks for longer periods, leading to increased output and higher quality work.

- **Improved Decision-Making:** A clear and focused mind fosters better decision-making and problem-solving abilities.

- **Reduced Stress and Anxiety:** Minimizing distractions promotes a calmer and more focused state of mind, leading to reduced stress levels.

- **Enhanced Creativity:** When you can work without distractions, your creativity flourishes, allowing you to generate innovative ideas.

- **Greater Job Satisfaction:** Feeling in control of your work environment and achieving goals leads to increased job satisfaction and motivation.

Apps & Settings: Your Digital Detox Arsenal:

Here's your toolkit to **silence the digital noise** and **reclaim your focus**:

- **Website Blockers:** Utilize website blockers to temporarily restrict access to distracting websites and social media platforms during focused work sessions. Popular options include Freedom, FocusMe, and Cold Turkey.

- **Focus Timers:** Employ focus timer apps like the Pomodoro Technique to break down work into focused intervals with short breaks in between. This promotes sustained focus and prevents mental fatigue. Popular options include Forest, Focus Keeper, and PomoDone.

- **Do Not Disturb Modes:** Utilize built-in "Do Not Disturb" modes on your phone and computer to silence notifications while working on important tasks.

- **Notification Management:** Customize notification settings on your phone and apps to limit distractions. Consider silencing all but essential notifications during focused work periods.

- **Email Management:** Schedule specific times to check emails and avoid the constant temptation to respond instantly. Consider using email automation tools to streamline communication.

- **Background Music Apps:** Utilize apps that provide focus-enhancing background music or ambient sounds to create a calming and productive work environment. Popular options include Focus@Will, Brain.fm, and Coffitivity.

- To-Do List and Task Management Apps: Utilize to-do list and task management apps to organize your workflow and prioritize tasks. This promotes focus and prevents feeling overwhelmed. Popular options include Todoist, Asana, and Trello.

Building Habits for a Focused Workflow:

Maintaining a distraction-free digital workspace requires ongoing effort:

- Experiment and Find What Works: Explore different apps and settings to identify what best suits your needs and preferences.

- Schedule Focused Work Sessions: Block out specific time slots in your calendar for focused work and utilize your chosen tools to minimize distractions during those periods.

- Communicate Proactively: Inform colleagues and clients when you'll be utilizing distraction-free tools and manage expectations regarding response times.

- Review Regularly: Periodically assess your use of apps and settings, ensuring they remain effective in minimizing distractions.

- Lead by Example: If you have a team, encourage them to explore similar tools and strategies to create a more focused work environment for everyone.

The Link Between Digital Focus and Increased Income:

By leveraging technology to minimize distractions, you're investing in yourself. Here's how it translates to increased income:

- **Increased Productivity:** More focused work translates to higher output and potentially increased earning potential.

- **Reduced Errors:** Improved focus leads to fewer errors, saving time and money spent on corrections.

- **Enhanced Client Satisfaction:** Focused work allows you to deliver high-quality work on time, leading to satisfied clients and repeat business.

- **Improved Time Management:** Less time wasted on distractions allows you to prioritize high-impact tasks and projects that contribute most to your income.

Identify and Eliminate Time-Sinks

Conquer the Scroll: Scheduling Breaks and Blocking Social Media for Peak Productivity and Income

The constant allure of social media can be a major productivity killer. But ditching your phone entirely isn't always the answer. The key lies in **strategic breaks** and **effective social media blocking tools**. This guide equips you with powerful strategies to **reclaim control of your attention**, **maximize your focus**, and unlock your peak earning potential.

The Pitfalls of Unmanaged Social Media:

Unrestricted access to social media can significantly hinder your performance:

- **Reduced Focus and Concentration:** Constant notifications and the temptation to scroll disrupt your thought process and erode attention spans.

- **Increased Time Wasted:** Checking social media feeds throughout the day can eat away at valuable work time.

- **Decision Fatigue:** The barrage of information and endless scrolling can lead to decision fatigue, hindering your ability to make sound judgments.

- **Increased Stress and Anxiety:** The pressure to keep up with social media and the fear of missing out can contribute to stress and anxiety.

- **Reduced Creativity:** Constant scrolling can stifle creativity and innovative thinking.

The Power of Strategic Breaks:

Scheduling short breaks throughout the workday offers a multitude of benefits:

- **Improved Focus and Concentration:** Short breaks allow your brain to refresh, leading to renewed focus and concentration upon returning to work.

- **Enhanced Creativity:** Breaks can spark new ideas and foster creative thinking.

- **Reduced Stress and Anxiety:** Taking time to step away from work can help manage stress and anxiety levels.

- **Increased Energy Levels:** Short breaks can help combat fatigue and boost energy levels.

- **Improved Overall Well-being:** Regular breaks promote physical and mental well-being, leading to increased productivity in the long run.

The Power of Social Media Blocking Tools:

Utilizing tools to block social media access during focused work sessions offers significant advantages:

- **Eliminate Distractions:** Blocking social media removes the constant temptation to scroll, allowing you to dedicate your full attention to work tasks.

- **Boost Productivity:** By eliminating distractions, you can accomplish more in less time with fewer interruptions.

- **Improved Time Management:** Blocking social media helps you stick to your schedule and avoid wasting time mindlessly scrolling.

- **Reduced Stress and Anxiety:** Knowing you're not accessible on social media can alleviate the pressure to constantly check in and reduce anxiety.

- **Enhanced Creativity:** Undistracted focus fosters creative thinking and problem-solving abilities.

Building a Focused Work Routine:

Here's your roadmap to **reclaim your attention** and **maximize your income**:

- **Schedule Focused Work Sessions:** Block out dedicated time slots in your calendar for focused work.

- **Utilize the Pomodoro Technique:** Break down your work into focused intervals (typically 25 minutes) with short breaks (typically 5 minutes) in between. Utilize apps like Forest or Focus Keeper to keep track of time.

- **Schedule Short Breaks:** Plan short breaks (ideally 2-5 minutes) throughout your focused work sessions to get up, move around, and refresh your mind. Consider using a timer app to remind yourself to take breaks.

- **Embrace Social Media Blocking Tools:** Explore and utilize apps and browser extensions like Freedom, Cold Turkey, or website blockers to restrict access to social media platforms during focused work sessions.

- **Turn Off Notifications:** Disable social media notifications on your phone and computer to avoid the constant temptation to check feeds.

- **Put Your Phone Away:** Consider putting your phone away in a drawer or silent mode during focused work sessions to minimize distractions.

- **Step Away From Your Desk:** During breaks, avoid using your phone or computer. Instead, stand up, stretch, walk around, or engage in a mindful activity like deep breathing exercises.

Building Habits for Long-Term Focus:

Maintaining a focused work routine requires ongoing effort:

- **Experiment and Find What Works:** Experiment with different break lengths and social media blocking tools to identify what best suits your needs and preferences.

- **Communicate with Colleagues and Clients:** Inform colleagues and clients about your focused work schedules and reduced social media availability during those times.

- **Review Regularly:** Periodically assess your social media usage and blocking strategies to ensure their effectiveness.

- **Reward Yourself:** Celebrate your successes in sticking to your schedule and minimizing distractions.

The Link Between Focus and Increased Income:

By leveraging strategic breaks and social media blocking tools, you're investing in yourself. Here's how it translates to increased income:

Increased Productivity: More focused work translates to higher output and potentially increased earning potential.

Reduced Errors: Improved focus leads to fewer errors, saving time and money spent on corrections.

- **Enhanced Creativity:** Regular breaks foster creative thinking, potentially leading to new ideas and innovations that can boost your income.

- **Improved Client Satisfaction:** Focused work allows you to deliver high-quality work on time, leading to satisfied clients.

Time Thieves Beware: Identifying and Eliminating Activities that Drain Your Productivity and Income

Time is a precious commodity, especially when it comes to maximizing your income potential. But **hidden time drains** lurk everywhere, eroding productivity and hindering your ability to achieve your goals. This guide equips you with powerful strategies to **identify** and **curb** these **time-wasting activities**, freeing up valuable time and boosting your earning potential.

The Culprits Behind Wasted Time:

Several activities can unknowingly steal your valuable work hours:

- **Unnecessary Multitasking:** Attempting to juggle multiple tasks simultaneously hinders focus and leads to errors, ultimately wasting time.

- **Unstructured Workflows:** A lack of planning and prioritization leads to inefficient workflows and wasted time spent on unimportant tasks.

- **Excessive Meetings:** Inefficient or poorly planned meetings can be significant time drains, disrupting your workflow.

- **Social Media Overuse:** Constant social media checking and scrolling can eat away at valuable work time.

- **Perfectionism:** The pursuit of perfection can lead to procrastination and hinder progress, ultimately wasting time.

- **Disorganization:** A cluttered workspace or disorganized digital files can waste time searching for information or resources.

- **Email Overload:** Constantly checking and responding to emails can disrupt your focus and lead to wasted time.

- **Unrealistic Deadlines:** Setting unrealistic deadlines can lead to stress, procrastination, and ultimately wasted time trying to catch up.

- **Interruptions:** Unwanted interruptions from colleagues or unexpected tasks can disrupt your workflow and waste time regaining focus.

- **Unnecessary Phone Calls:** Long, unproductive phone calls can steal valuable work time.

The Power of Identifying Your Time Drains:

By recognizing your personal time-wasting activities, you unlock the ability to:

- **Increase Productivity:** Eliminating time-wasting activities frees up valuable time for focused work, leading to increased output.

- **Reduce Stress and Anxiety:** Feeling in control of your time reduces stress and allows you to focus on important tasks with a clear mind.

- **Improve Work-Life Balance:** Reclaimed time allows you to dedicate more time to personal life and activities you enjoy.

- **Enhanced Decision-Making:** Reduced stress and a clearer head promote better decision-making.

- **Greater Job Satisfaction:** Feeling productive and accomplishing goals leads to increased job satisfaction and motivation.

Strategies for Pinpointing Your Time Drains:

Here's your action plan to **identify your personal time thieves**:

- **Track Your Time:** Utilize time tracking apps or a simple log to monitor how you spend your work hours. Identify recurring activities that consume significant chunks of time.

- **Analyze Your Workday:** Reflect on your typical workday and identify moments when you feel your focus waning or time slipping away.

- **Review Your Calendar:** Assess your calendar to identify time slots filled with unproductive meetings or activities you can streamline.

- **Listen to Your Body:** Pay attention to your energy levels throughout the day. Activities that drain your energy are likely time drains.

- **Seek Feedback:** Ask colleagues or a trusted mentor for feedback on your work habits. They may identify areas where you unknowingly waste time.

Curbing the Time-Wasting Activities:

Once you've identified your time drains, equip yourself with **strategies to eliminate or minimize them**:

- **Prioritize ruthlessly:** Focus on the most important tasks (high-impact activities) and delegate or eliminate less important ones.

- **Embrace Time Management Techniques:** Utilize time management tools like the Eisenhower Matrix or the Pomodoro Technique to structure your workday and prioritize tasks effectively.

- **Schedule Meetings Strategically:** Set clear agendas, keep meetings short, and limit attendance to necessary participants.

- **Manage Social Media Access:** Utilize social media blocking tools during focused work sessions and schedule specific times for checking social media.

- **Combat Perfectionism:** Set realistic goals and deadlines, and accept that "good enough" might be sufficient in some cases.

- **Organize Your Workspace and Digital Files:** Invest time in organizing your physical workspace and digital files to minimize time spent searching for information.

- **Batch Similar Tasks:** Group similar tasks together to minimize context switching and improve efficiency.

- **Learn to Say No:** Don't overload your schedule with additional tasks or meetings that would significantly disrupt your workflow.

- **Communicate Clear Boundaries:** Inform colleagues and clients about your work hours and preferred communication methods to minimize interruptions.

- **Delegate When Possible:** Don't be afraid to delegate tasks that can be handled by others, freeing up your time for focused work.

Building Habits for Lasting Productivity:

Maintaining efficient time management requires ongoing effort:

- **Review Regularly:** Periodically assess your time management strategies and identify areas for improvement.

- **Communicate Proactively:** Inform colleagues and clients about your work style and preferred communication methods to minimize disruptions.

- **Reward Yourself:** Celebrate your successes in reclaiming control of your time and boosting your productivity.

- **Seek Support:** If you struggle with time management, consider time management coaching or workshops for additional guidance.

The Link Between Time Management and Increased Income:

- **Increased Productivity:** The core benefit of time management is maximizing your output within a set timeframe. Focused work sessions and streamlined workflows lead to completing more high-value tasks, directly impacting your earning potential. Imagine completing an extra project or exceeding client expectations – that translates to increased pay or attracting new clients.

- **Reduced Errors:** Haste often leads to mistakes. Time management allows for careful planning and execution, minimizing errors. This translates to less time spent fixing mistakes and rework, freeing you up for more income-generating activities. Consider the cost of revisions or corrections in your field – time management helps you avoid those expenses.

- **Improved Client Satisfaction:** Delivering high-quality work on time is key to client satisfaction. Time management ensures you meet deadlines consistently, exceeding client expectations. Satisfied clients are more likely to become repeat clients or recommend your services to others, leading to a sustainable income stream.

- **Enhanced Time Management Skills Signal Value:** Strong time management skills are highly sought after in today's workforce. They demonstrate your ability to prioritize tasks, work independently, and deliver results efficiently. This can give you a competitive edge when negotiating salaries or seeking promotions, potentially leading to a higher income bracket.

- **Reduced Stress and Burnout:** Feeling overwhelmed by a never-ending to-do list can lead to stress and burnout. Effective time management prevents this by providing a sense of control and clarity. You'll be able to tackle tasks efficiently, reducing stress and allowing you to sustain your peak performance for longer periods, ultimately leading to a higher income over time.

- **More Time for Income-Generating Activities:** By streamlining your workflow and eliminating time-wasting activities, you free up valuable time to dedicate to income-generating activities. This could involve taking on additional projects, developing new skills to expand your service offerings, or networking to attract new clients.

Remember, time management is a skill that requires continuous practice. By implementing the strategies outlined above and consistently monitoring your progress, you'll be well on your way to unlocking your full earning potential.

Track Your Progress and Celebrate Milestones

Apps and Journals for Tracking Progress

Taming the To-Do List: Tracking Progress with Time Management Apps and Bullet Journals

The road to achieving your goals is paved with good intentions, but staying on track often requires a roadmap. Enter **time management apps** and **bullet journals**, powerful tools to **monitor your progress, stay organized**, and **maximize your productivity**. This guide dives into the strengths of each approach, helping you choose the one that best suits your style and needs.

The Power of Progress Tracking:

Monitoring your progress offers a multitude of benefits:

- **Increased Motivation:** Seeing tangible progress visually reinforces your goals and motivates you to keep pushing forward.

- **Improved Focus:** Tracking your progress allows you to identify areas that require more attention and adjust your strategies accordingly.

- **Enhanced Accountability:** By documenting your progress, you hold yourself accountable for achieving your goals.

- **Boosted Confidence:** Witnessing your progress fosters a sense of accomplishment and boosts your confidence.

- **Better Decision-Making:** Data collected through progress tracking allows you to analyze your workflow and make informed decisions about resource allocation and time management.

Digital Organization: Time Management Apps

Time management apps offer a plethora of features to **track your progress** in a digital format:

- **Goal Setting and Tracking:** Set specific, measurable, achievable, relevant, and time-bound (SMART) goals and track your progress towards them through various features like progress bars, milestone markers, and achievement badges. Popular options include Asana, Todoist, and Trello.

- **Task Management and Scheduling:** Break down large projects into smaller, manageable tasks, assign deadlines, and schedule them on calendar interfaces. Track your progress on each task and visualize your overall workflow. Popular options include Microsoft To Do, Google Tasks, and Evernote.

- **Habit Tracking:** Build positive habits and monitor their consistency with habit tracking features. Many apps offer streak counters, reminders, and motivational quotes to support habit formation. Popular options include Forest, Habitica, and Fabulous.

- **Data Analysis and Reporting:** Some apps generate reports and insights based on your progress data, allowing you to identify trends and areas for improvement. This data-driven approach can inform your future goal setting and time management strategies. Popular options include Toggl Track, RescueTime, and Clockify.

The Tactile Touch: Bullet Journals

For those who prefer a more hands-on approach, **bullet journals** offer a customizable and visually stimulating way to **track progress**:

- **Flexibility and Customization:** Bullet journals are essentially blank notebooks that you can personalize according to your needs. Create layouts for daily to-do lists, weekly trackers, habit trackers, and project planning pages.

- **Visual Appeal:** Doodling, color-coding, and using creative layouts can make your bullet journal visually engaging, promoting both progress tracking and enjoyment.

- **Mindfulness and Focus:** The act of writing down your goals and tasks can improve focus and retention compared to relying solely on digital tools.

- **Mind Mapping:** Use mind maps to visually brainstorm ideas, track project progress, and connect related tasks. This approach can be particularly helpful for visual thinkers.

- **Minimal Tech Dependence:** Bullet journals offer a tech-free way to track progress and organize your thoughts. This can be beneficial for those who experience digital fatigue or want to disconnect from technology for periods.

Choosing the Right Tool for You:

Here are some pointers to help you decide which approach aligns best with your preferences:

- **Tech-Savvy vs. Analog:** Do you prefer the convenience of digital tools or the tactile experience of a physical notebook?

- **Visual Learner:** If visual elements motivate you, a bullet journal's creative freedom might be ideal.

- **Organization Style:** Consider whether you thrive on a pre-structured app environment or a customizable bullet journal layout.

- **Accessibility Needs:** If you require accessibility features like voice input or screen readers, a time management app might be more suitable.

Maximizing Your Progress Journey:

Whichever method you choose, here are some tips to ensure success:

- **Set SMART Goals:** Clearly define your goals to track progress effectively.

- **Regular Reviews:** Schedule regular reviews to assess your progress, identify challenges, and adjust your strategies.

- **Celebrate Milestones:** Acknowledge and celebrate your achievements along the way to maintain motivation.

- **Personalize Your System:** Adapt your chosen approach to fit your needs and preferences.

- **Consistency is Key:** Regularly update your progress tracker, whether it's a digital app or your bullet journal, for accurate data and a clear picture of your progress.

By **monitoring your progress**, you gain valuable insights into your work habits and stay motivated on the path to achieving your goals.

See Your Success: The Power of Visualization for Accomplishment and Growth

We all strive for success, but the journey can feel overwhelming without a clear roadmap.

Visualization is a powerful tool that allows you to **see your accomplishments** and **identify areas for improvement**, guiding you towards your goals with renewed clarity and focus. This guide explores the benefits of visualization and equips you with effective strategies to **harness its potential**.

The Power of Visualization:

Visualization is the act of creating mental images of your desired outcomes. This mental rehearsal offers a multitude of benefits:

- **Increased Motivation:** Seeing yourself achieving your goals fosters a sense of belief and motivates you to take action.

- **Enhanced Focus:** A clear mental picture of your goals helps you prioritize tasks and avoid distractions.

- **Improved Confidence:** Visualizing success builds your confidence in your abilities to achieve your goals.

- **Boosted Creativity:** The visualization process can spark new ideas and innovative approaches to problem-solving.

- **Reduced Stress and Anxiety:** Focusing on positive outcomes can alleviate stress and anxiety associated with achieving goals.

- **Identification of Potential Challenges:** Through visualization, you can anticipate potential roadblocks and develop strategies to overcome them.

Visualizing Your Accomplishments:

Here's how to **harness the power of visualization** to celebrate your achievements:

- **Create a Vision Board:** Physically manifest your goals by creating a vision board with images, quotes, and affirmations that represent your desired outcomes. Visually seeing your goals can serve as a constant source of motivation.

- **Journal Your Successes:** Take time to reflect and write down your accomplishments, both big and small. Recording your progress reinforces your sense of accomplishment and motivates you to keep striving.

- **Celebrate Milestones:** Take time to acknowledge and celebrate your milestones. This reinforces positive associations with achieving goals and motivates you to continue on your journey.

- **Visualization Exercises:** Close your eyes and visualize yourself successfully completing a task or achieving a goal. Focus on the positive emotions associated with success. Engage all your senses in this visualization for a more immersive experience.

Identifying Areas for Improvement Through Visualization:

Visualization isn't just about celebrating success; it's also about identifying growth opportunities:

- **Visualize Facing Challenges:** Imagine potential obstacles you might encounter on your path to achieving your goals. Visualize yourself overcoming these challenges and develop strategies to mitigate them in real life.

- **Gap Analysis:** Visually compare your current situation with your desired outcome. This identifies areas where you need to focus your efforts.

- **Visualization Exercises:** Imagine yourself struggling with a specific task or facing a particular weakness. Analyze the visualization and identify areas where you can improve.

Strategies for Effective Visualization:

Here are some tips for **maximizing the effectiveness of your visualizations**:

- **Clarity is Key:** The more vivid and detailed your visualizations, the more impactful they will be. Engage your senses (sight, sound, touch, smell) to create a realistic mental picture.

- **Positive Emotions:** Focus on the positive emotions associated with achieving your goals. This emotional connection fuels motivation and strengthens the visualization.

- **Regular Practice:** The benefits of visualization compound with consistent practice. Schedule regular time to visualize your goals and progress.
- **Combine with Action:** Visualization is a powerful tool, but it's not a substitute for action. Use your visualizations to inform your actions and develop a clear roadmap to achieve your goals.
- **Be Patient:** Achieving goals takes time and effort. Don't be discouraged if you don't see immediate results. Maintain a positive mindset and trust in the power of visualization.

Visualizing Your Path to Success

By **harnessing the power of visualization**, you gain a powerful tool to **track your progress**, **identify areas for improvement**, and **stay motivated** on your journey towards achieving your goals. Remember, visualization is a **personal practice**. Experiment with different techniques and find what works best for you. With consistent effort and a positive mindset, you can turn your visualizations into reality.

The Fuel for Success: Maintaining Motivation and Aligning Your Efforts with Your Goals

The path to achieving your goals is rarely a straight line. Motivation can ebb and flow, and distractions can pull you off course. However, by employing **strategies to maintain motivation** and

aligning your efforts with your aspirations, you can navigate challenges and **transform your goals into reality.** This guide equips you with powerful tools and techniques to **stay focused, inspired, and on track** for long-term success.

The Elusive Flame of Motivation:

Maintaining motivation is crucial for sustained effort towards your goals. Here's why it can be a challenge:

- **Setbacks and Challenges:** Encountering obstacles can lead to discouragement and a decline in motivation.

- **Loss of Focus:** Daily distractions and competing priorities can divert your attention from your goals.

- **Lack of Progress:** If you don't see immediate results, you might feel discouraged and lose motivation.

- **Fear of Failure:** The fear of failure can paralyze you and prevent you from taking action.

Strategies to Reignite Your Motivational Fire:

Here are some techniques to **rekindle your motivation** and keep it burning brightly:

- **Reconnect with Your "Why":** Remind yourself of the deeper reasons behind your goals. What are you passionate about? What impact do you want to achieve? Rekindling that initial spark can reignite your motivation.

- **Set SMART Goals:** Clearly defined Specific, Measurable, Achievable, Relevant, and Time-bound (SMART) goals provide a roadmap and a sense of direction. Track your progress towards these goals to celebrate milestones and stay motivated.

- **Break Down Large Goals:** Large, overwhelming goals can be daunting. Break them down into smaller, manageable steps. Completing these smaller tasks provides a sense of accomplishment and fuels motivation to keep going.

- **Visualize Success:** Engage in visualization exercises. See yourself achieving your goals and experiencing the positive emotions associated with success. This mental rehearsal reinforces your belief in your ability to achieve your goals.

- **Reward Yourself:** Celebrate your achievements, big and small. Rewarding yourself reinforces positive behavior and keeps you motivated to continue progressing.

- **Find a Support System:** Surround yourself with positive and supportive people who believe in you and your goals. Their encouragement can be a powerful source of motivation.

- **Focus on Progress, Not Perfection:** Don't get bogged down by striving for perfection. Focus on making consistent progress, even if it's in small increments.

- **Embrace Challenges:** View challenges as opportunities for growth. Learning from setbacks can strengthen your resolve and make you a more resilient individual.

Aligning Your Efforts: Goals Take Center Stage:

Once motivated, ensure your actions are **aligned** with your goals:

- **Prioritization is Key:** Identify the most important tasks that move you closer to your goals. Focus on high-impact activities and delegate or eliminate less important ones.

- **Time Management Techniques:** Utilize time management tools and techniques like the Eisenhower Matrix or the Pomodoro Technique to structure your workday and prioritize tasks effectively.

- **Say No to Distractions:** Learn to decline requests that don't align with your goals. Protect your time and focus on activities that contribute to your progress.

- **Schedule Focused Work Sessions:** Block out dedicated time slots in your calendar for focused work on your most important tasks. Minimize distractions during these sessions.

- **Regular Reviews:** Schedule regular check-ins to assess your progress and ensure your actions remain aligned with your goals. This allows for course correction if necessary.

- **Embrace Continuous Learning:** Constantly seek new knowledge and skills that support your goals. This ongoing learning keeps you engaged and motivated.

Building Habits for Long-Term Success:

Maintaining motivation and alignment with your goals requires ongoing effort:

- **Develop a Growth Mindset:** Believe in your ability to learn and grow. View challenges as opportunities to develop new skills and become a better version of yourself.

- **Celebrate the Journey, Not Just the Destination:** Enjoy the process of working towards your goals. Focus on the learning and growth that occurs along the way.

- **Practice Gratitude:** Take time to appreciate your progress and the positive aspects of your journey. Gratitude fosters a positive mindset and fuels motivation.

- **Be Kind to Yourself:** Don't beat yourself up for occasional setbacks. Learn from mistakes, forgive yourself, and recommit to your goals.

The Road to Success is Paved with Motivation and Alignment

By reigniting your motivation and aligning your efforts, you create a powerful formula for success. Remember, the journey towards your goals is a marathon, not a sprint. With unwavering determination, strategic planning, and a commitment to self-care, you can overcome challenges, stay focused, and achieve your full potential.

Reward Yourself for Reaching Milestones

The Power of Positive Reinforcement: Rewarding Yourself for Milestones and Completed Tasks

The road to achieving goals can be long and challenging. While intrinsic motivation – the desire to achieve for personal satisfaction – is crucial, extrinsic motivators – external rewards – can play a powerful role in keeping you focused and energized. **Rewarding yourself** for reaching milestones and completing tasks is a powerful strategy to **boost motivation, reinforce positive behavior,** and **accelerate your progress**. This guide explores the benefits of self-rewards and equips you with creative ideas to **celebrate your achievements** along the way.

The Science Behind Self-Rewards:

Self-rewards tap into the power of **positive reinforcement**. When you complete a task or reach a milestone, rewarding yourself creates a positive association with that accomplishment. This association triggers the release of dopamine, a neurotransmitter associated with pleasure and motivation. As a result, you're more likely to repeat the desired behavior (completing tasks) in pursuit of that positive reinforcement (the reward) in the future.

Benefits of Rewarding Yourself:

Here's how strategically celebrating your achievements can benefit your journey:

- **Increased Motivation:** Knowing a reward awaits you at the finish line can motivate you to push through challenges and persist in your efforts.

- **Enhanced Focus:** The anticipation of a reward can help you stay focused on the task at hand and avoid distractions.

- **Improved Performance:** Self-rewards can boost your performance by increasing your energy levels and engagement.

- **Positive Reinforcement:** Rewarding yourself reinforces positive behavior, making it more likely you'll continue the actions that lead to your goals.

- **Greater Sense of Accomplishment:** Celebrating milestones amplifies your sense of accomplishment, fostering confidence and keeping you motivated.

Crafting Effective Rewards:

Here are some key elements for crafting **effective self-rewards**:

- **Meaningful and Motivating:** Choose rewards that are personally meaningful to you and motivate you to keep moving forward. A reward that feels like a chore won't be effective.

- **Aligned with Your Goals:** Ensure your rewards don't undermine your overall goals. For example, if your goal is to eat healthier, don't reward yourself with unhealthy food.

- **Varied and Proportional:** Utilize a variety of rewards to maintain novelty and excitement. Tailor the reward to the significance of the achievement. A small milestone might warrant a smaller reward, while a major milestone deserves a more significant celebration.

Reward Ideas for Every Milestone:

Here's a diverse selection of reward ideas to **celebrate your achievements**:

- **Experiences:** Treat yourself to a movie night, a concert ticket, a museum visit, or a weekend getaway.

- **Self-Care:** Indulge in a relaxing bath, get a massage, or schedule a spa day.

- **Personal Development:** Invest in a new book or online course related to your interests or goals.

- **Hobbies and Entertainment:** Spend time on your favorite hobbies, play video games, or watch a TV show you enjoy.

- **Food and Drinks:** Enjoy your favorite meal or beverage, try a new restaurant, or indulge in a sweet treat.

- **Material Rewards:** Purchase a small item you've been eyeing, treat yourself to new clothes, or invest in a productivity tool that will enhance your work.

- **Social Rewards:** Connect with friends and family, celebrate with a loved one, or plan a fun outing with colleagues.

- **Digital Rewards:** Download a new app or game you've been wanting to try, watch a movie on a streaming platform you rarely use, or buy a new song or audiobook.

- **Time Off:** Take a break from work, enjoy a long lunch, or simply relax and do nothing.

Building a Sustainable Reward System:

Here are some tips for **integrating self-rewards** into your goal-achievement strategy:

- **Set Clear Milestones:** Define clear milestones along your journey to identify moments deserving of reward.

- **Plan Your Rewards in Advance:** Decide on potential rewards for different milestones beforehand to avoid impulsive choices that might undermine your goals.

- **Don't Overdo It:** Avoid over-rewarding yourself for small tasks. Save the bigger rewards for significant milestones to maintain their motivational impact.

- **Focus on Progress, Not Perfection:** Reward yourself for consistent progress, not just achieving perfection. This fosters a growth mindset and keeps you motivated.

- **Focus on the Journey:** While rewards are a valuable tool, remember to celebrate the process of working towards your goals, not just the end result.

By **rewarding yourself strategically** for reaching milestones and completing tasks, you create a powerful feedback loop that **boosts motivation, reinforces positive behavior**, and keeps you **engaged in your journey towards success**. Remember, self-rewards are an investment in yourself and your goals. Choose rewards that bring you joy and fuel your progress!

Fan the Flames of Progress: Reinforcing Positive Behavior and Maintaining Enthusiasm

The road to achieving your goals is paved with good intentions, but staying motivated and consistent requires more than just a strong desire. **Reinforcing positive behavior** and **maintaining enthusiasm** are crucial ingredients for long-term success. This guide equips you with powerful strategies to **celebrate your wins, fuel your motivation**, and **transform your goals from aspirations to reality**.

The Power of Positive Reinforcement:

When it comes to building habits and achieving goals, positive reinforcement is your secret weapon. It's a psychological principle where rewarding desired behaviors increases the likelihood of repeating them. Here's how it works:

- **Dopamine Release:** Positive reinforcement triggers the release of dopamine, a neurotransmitter associated with pleasure and reward. This creates a positive association with the desired behavior.

- **Enhanced Motivation:** The anticipation of a reward motivates you to push through challenges and persist in your efforts.

- **Improved Performance:** Positive reinforcement can boost your performance by increasing your energy levels and engagement.

Reinforcing Positive Behavior for Success:

Here are some key strategies to leverage positive reinforcement for achieving your goals:

- **Identify Your Goals:** Clearly define your goals to understand the behaviors you need to reinforce.

- **Set SMART Goals:** Make your goals Specific, Measurable, Achievable, Relevant, and Time-bound (SMART). This allows you to identify milestones that deserve celebration.

- **Break Down Large Goals:** Divide large, daunting goals into smaller, manageable steps. Celebrating completing these smaller steps keeps you motivated and reinforces positive progress.

- **Reward Yourself:** Choose meaningful and motivating rewards for achieving milestones. These rewards should be aligned with your values and not undermine your overall goals.

- **Track Your Progress:** Monitor your progress towards your goals. This allows you to identify areas for improvement and celebrate achievements along the way.

- **Focus on the Positive:** Instead of dwelling on setbacks, focus on the positive steps you've taken and the progress you've made.

Maintaining Enthusiasm for the Long Haul:

Enthusiasm is the spark that ignites your journey. Here's how to **keep the flames burning bright**:

- **Reconnect with Your "Why":** Remind yourself of the deeper reasons behind your goals. What excites you about achieving them? Reconnecting with your purpose can reignite your enthusiasm.

- **Visualize Success:** Engage in visualization exercises. Imagine yourself achieving your goals and experiencing the positive emotions associated with success. This mental rehearsal reinforces your motivation and keeps you enthusiastic.

- **Celebrate Your Wins:** Take time to acknowledge and celebrate your achievements, big and small. This reinforces a sense of accomplishment and keeps you motivated to keep moving forward.

- **Surround Yourself with Positivity:** Seek out supportive people who believe in you and your goals. Their positive energy can be contagious and help you stay enthusiastic.

- **Embrace Challenges:** View challenges as opportunities to learn and grow. Overcoming hurdles strengthens your resolve and fuels your enthusiasm for achieving your goals.

- **Practice Gratitude:** Take time to appreciate your progress and the positive aspects of your journey. Gratitude fosters a positive mindset and fuels enthusiasm.

- **Reward Yourself for Maintaining Enthusiasm:** Just as you reward yourself for completing tasks, consider **rewarding** yourself for maintaining a positive attitude. Treat yourself to something you enjoy for staying motivated and focused.

Building Habits for Lasting Change:

Reinforcing positive behavior and maintaining enthusiasm requires ongoing effort:

- **Develop a Growth Mindset:** Believe in your ability to learn and grow. View setbacks as opportunities to develop new skills and become a better version of yourself.

- **Focus on Progress, Not Perfection:** Don't get discouraged by striving for perfection. Focus on making consistent progress, even if it's in small increments.

- **Practice Self-Care:** Prioritize your physical and mental well-being. Taking care of yourself ensures you have the energy and resilience to stay enthusiastic and achieve your goals.

- **Embrace Continuous Learning:** Constantly seek new knowledge and skills that support your goals. This ongoing learning keeps you engaged and enthusiastic about your journey.

By **reinforcing positive behavior** and **maintaining enthusiasm**, you transform your goals from aspirations to a **thriving reality**. Celebrate your wins, embrace challenges, and **enjoy the journey** of becoming the best version of yourself.

Building Your Productivity Powerhouse: A Sustainable System for Long-Term Gains

Productivity isn't just about squeezing more tasks into your day; it's about **optimizing your workflow** to achieve **consistent, high-quality results**. But maintaining peak productivity over the long haul requires a **sustainable system**. This guide equips you with the tools and strategies to **build a productivity powerhouse** that fuels your success **without burning you out**.

The Pillars of Sustainable Productivity:

A sustainable productivity system rests on four key pillars:

- **Goal Alignment:** Ensure your efforts are directed towards goals that are meaningful and aligned with your values. This intrinsic motivation fuels long-term commitment.

- **Effective Planning & Prioritization:** Clearly define your goals and break them down into manageable tasks. Prioritize these tasks strategically to focus on high-impact activities first.

- **Optimized Workflow & Time Management:** Implement strategies like time blocking, task batching, and the Eisenhower Matrix to structure your workday and minimize distractions.

- **Self-Care & Well-Being:** Prioritize your physical and mental well-being. Getting enough sleep, maintaining a healthy diet, and practicing stress management techniques boost your energy and focus, allowing you to sustain high productivity levels.

Building Your System: Step-by-Step

Here's a step-by-step approach to **crafting your sustainable productivity system**:

Identify Your Values and Goals: Reflect on your values and aspirations. What do you want to achieve in life? Define SMART goals that align with these values and keep you motivated.

- **Embrace Time Management Techniques:** Explore time management strategies like the Eisenhower Matrix, the Pomodoro Technique, and time blocking. Experiment and find techniques that maximize your focus and minimize distractions.

- **Craft a Personalized Schedule:** Create a daily or weekly schedule that incorporates dedicated work sessions, breaks, time for self-care, and other commitments. Ensure your schedule is realistic and allows for flexibility.

- **Prioritize Ruthlessly:** Not all tasks are created equal. Learn to prioritize ruthlessly, focusing on high-impact activities that move you closer to your goals. Delegate or eliminate less important tasks.

- **Embrace Automation:** Utilize technology to automate repetitive tasks. This frees up valuable time and energy for more strategic work.

- **Minimize Distractions:** Identify your biggest distractions (social media, email notifications) and develop strategies to minimize their impact. Consider using website blockers or silencing notifications during focused work sessions.

- **Create a Positive Work Environment:** Designate a workspace that is organized, clutter-free, and conducive to focused work. Personalize your workspace to create a positive and inspiring environment.

- **Prioritize Sleep and Well-Being:** Getting enough sleep is crucial for optimal cognitive function and productivity. Maintain a healthy diet, exercise regularly, and practice stress management techniques to boost your energy and resilience.

- **Schedule Regular Reviews:** Regularly evaluate your productivity system. Identify areas for improvement and make adjustments as needed. Your system should be adaptable to your evolving needs and goals.

- **Celebrate Milestones:** Acknowledge and celebrate your progress. Rewarding yourself for achieving milestones reinforces positive behavior and keeps you motivated on your journey.

Additional Tips for Long-Term Success:

- Embrace Continuous Learning: Continuously expand your knowledge and skills related to your goals. This keeps your work engaging and fuels long-term motivation.

- Find a Productivity Buddy: Partner with a colleague or friend who shares similar goals. Hold each other accountable and share tips and tricks for staying productive.

- Practice Mindfulness: Mindfulness techniques like meditation can improve your focus, reduce stress, and enhance your overall well-being, leading to sustained productivity gains.

Remember: Sustainability is Key

The key to long-term success is building a **system that works for you** and that you can **maintain over time**. Avoid falling into the trap of unsustainable productivity hacks that lead to burnout. Focus on creating a system that **supports your well-being** while propelling you towards your goals.

Conclusion

Recap of the 10 Powerful Productivity Hacks

10 Powerful Productivity Hacks to Boost Your Income

Feeling overwhelmed by your to-do list? Struggling to find the time (and focus) to reach your full earning potential? Don't worry, we've all been there. But the good news is, **increased productivity** is directly linked to **increased income**. By implementing these 10 powerful productivity hacks, you can streamline your workflow, maximize your output, and ultimately **boost your income**.

1. Time Management Mastery: Effective time management allows you to **accomplish more** within a set timeframe. Utilize time management techniques like scheduling, prioritization, and batching similar tasks to free up valuable time for income-generating activities.

2. Reduced Errors: Haste often leads to mistakes. Time management fosters **careful planning and execution**, minimizing errors and rework. This translates to less time spent fixing mistakes and more time dedicated to billable hours or income-generating projects.

3. **Enhanced Client Satisfaction:** Delivering high-quality work on time is key to client satisfaction. Time management ensures you **meet deadlines consistently**, exceeding client expectations and fostering repeat business or referrals - leading to a more **sustainable income stream**.

4. **Time Management Signals Value:** Strong time management skills are highly sought after in today's workforce. They demonstrate your ability to **prioritize tasks, work independently, and deliver results efficiently**. This can give you a competitive edge when **negotiating salaries** or **seeking promotions**, potentially leading to a higher income bracket.

5. **Reduced Stress and Burnout:** Feeling overwhelmed by a never-ending to-do list can lead to stress and burnout. Effective time management prevents this by providing a sense of control and clarity. You'll be able to **tackle tasks efficiently**, reducing stress and allowing you to **sustain your peak performance** for longer periods, ultimately leading to a higher income over time.

6. **More Time for Income-Generating Activities:** By streamlining your workflow and

eliminating time-wasting activities, you free up valuable time. Dedicate this newfound time to activities that directly generate income, such as taking on additional projects, developing new skills to expand your service offerings, or networking to attract new clients.

7. **Harness the Power of Technology:** Leverage technology to your advantage. Utilize **time management apps** to track your progress, schedule tasks, and stay organized. Explore **communication tools** to collaborate efficiently with clients and colleagues. Consider **productivity software** specifically designed for your field to streamline workflows and save time.

8. **Create a Dedicated Workspace:** Having a designated workspace, free from distractions, can significantly **improve your focus** and **boost your productivity**. This can be a physical space in your home or office, or a virtual workspace created through software.

9. **The Power of Planning:** Taking time to plan your workday or week in advance allows you to **prioritize tasks**, **allocate time effectively**, and **anticipate potential challenges**. This proactive approach ensures you're working on the most important tasks at the right time, maximizing your productivity and income potential.

10. **Track Your Progress and Celebrate Wins:** Monitoring your progress allows you to see the tangible results of your efforts. It also helps you identify areas for improvement. Regularly track your accomplishments, no matter how small, and **celebrate your wins**. This motivates you to stay on track and reinforces positive behavior.

By implementing these 10 powerful productivity hacks, you can **transform your time management skills, boost your efficiency**, and ultimately **unlock your full earning potential**. Remember, **consistency is key**. The more you practice these strategies, the more natural they will become, leading to long-term success and a healthier, more productive work life.

The Road to Earning More with Increased Efficiency and Time Management

The Road to Earning More: Efficiency and Time Management for Financial Success

Have you ever felt like there just aren't enough hours in the day to achieve your financial goals? You're not alone. Many people struggle with balancing work, personal lives, and the pursuit of a higher income. But the truth is, **earning more doesn't always require working harder**. It's about working **smarter**. Here's how **increased** efficiency and **effective time management** can pave the way for greater financial success.

Why Efficiency and Time Management Matter:

- **Maximize Your Time:** There are only 24 hours in a day. Effective time management ensures you spend those hours on high-impact activities that directly contribute to your income.

- **Minimize Time-Wasters:** Emails, social media, and distractions can eat away at valuable time. Time management helps you identify and eliminate distractions, allowing you to focus on income-generating tasks.

- **Boost Productivity:** When you work efficiently, you accomplish more in less time. This translates to increased output, whether measured by billable hours, completed projects, or sales.

- **Reduce Stress and Burnout:** Feeling constantly overwhelmed can lead to stress and burnout, hindering your productivity and motivation. Effective time management creates a **sense of control** and allows you to **work strategically**, reducing stress and promoting sustained performance.

- **Enhanced Client Satisfaction:** Meeting deadlines consistently and delivering high-quality work is essential for client satisfaction. Time management ensures you can manage client expectations effectively, leading to repeat business and referrals – a stable foundation for a healthy income.

Building Your Efficiency and Time Management Toolkit:

Here are some key strategies to **transform your work habits** and **unlock your earning potential**:

- **Goal Setting and Prioritization:** Define your **financial goals**. What do you want to achieve? Once you have a clear vision, set SMART goals (Specific, Measurable, Achievable, Relevant, and Time-bound) that break down your larger objectives into actionable steps.

- **Time Management Techniques:** Explore tools like scheduling, timeboxing (allocating specific time slots for tasks), and to-do lists. Consider the Eisenhower Matrix for prioritizing tasks based on urgency and importance.

- **Minimize Distractions:** Silence notifications, turn off social media, and find a quiet workspace to minimize interruptions. Utilize tools like website blockers or apps that promote focused work.

- **Batch Similar Tasks:** Group similar tasks together to improve focus and reduce context switching. Instead of jumping between emails and calls, schedule dedicated times for each activity.

- **Embrace Technology:** Leverage productivity apps to manage your time, schedule tasks, and collaborate with clients. Utilize communication tools for efficient communication, saving you time and frustration.

- **Delegate or Outsource:** Identify tasks that can be delegated to colleagues or outsourced to freelancers. Free up your valuable time to focus on high-impact activities that directly contribute to your income.

- **Track Your Progress and Analyze Data:** Monitor your progress towards your goals. Track your time spent on various activities and identify areas for improvement. Analyze your data to understand what works best for you and adjust your strategies accordingly.

- **Automate Repetitive Tasks:** Many repetitive tasks can be automated through technology. Explore tools that can automate scheduling appointments, sending emails, or data entry.

- **Invest in Yourself:** Continuously learn and develop new skills to increase your value in the marketplace. This can involve attending workshops, taking courses, or reading industry publications.

- **Create a Dedicated Workspace:** Having a designated workspace, free from distractions, can improve your focus and boost your productivity.

- **Schedule Breaks for Self-Care:** Schedule regular breaks to avoid burnout and maintain a positive and focused mindset. Taking care of yourself ensures you have the energy and resilience needed for sustained performance.

Remember, Building Efficiency is an Ongoing Process:

- **Start Small and Gradually Increase:** Don't overwhelm yourself with an entirely new system at once. Implement changes gradually and allow yourself time to adjust.

- **Find Your Flow:** Experiment with different techniques and tools to discover what works best for you and your work style.

- **Celebrate Your Wins:** Acknowledge your progress and celebrate your achievements, no matter how small. This reinforces positive behavior and keeps you motivated.

- **Be Flexible and Adaptable:** Be prepared to adjust your strategies as your goals and circumstances change.

Embracing Continuous Improvement and Refining Your Strategies

The Ascent of Excellence: Embracing Continuous Improvement and Refining Your Strategies

The path to success is rarely a straight line. It's a winding journey paved with challenges, triumphs, and lessons learned. **Continuous improvement**, a core principle adopted by high achievers, equips you to **navigate this journey effectively**. By embracing **continuous improvement** and refining **your strategies**, you can **transform setbacks into stepping stones** and **steadily ascend towards excellence.**

Why Embrace Continuous Improvement?

The world around us is constantly evolving. **Continuous improvement** acknowledges this dynamism and provides a framework for **adapting and thriving** in a changing landscape. Here's why it matters:

Maintaining Your Competitive Edge: In today's competitive environment, complacency is your enemy. **Continuous improvement** ensures you **stay ahead of the curve** by constantly learning, adapting, and refining your approach.

- **Unleashing Your Full Potential:** There's always room for growth. Continuous improvement fosters a growth mindset, pushing you to exceed your limitations and reach your full potential.

- **Transforming Setbacks into Opportunities:** Challenges are inevitable. Continuous improvement equips you to view setbacks as learning experiences instead of failures. You can analyze mistakes, refine your strategies, and emerge stronger.

- **Boosting Motivation and Engagement:** Seeing consistent progress is motivating. Continuous improvement keeps you engaged and inspired by the constant pursuit of excellence.

- **Building Resilience:** The road to success is not without obstacles. Continuous improvement fosters resilience by equipping you to bounce back from challenges and adapt to changing circumstances.

The Art of Refining Your Strategies:

- **Continuous improvement** isn't just about action; it's about strategic action. Here's how to refine your strategies for optimal results:

- **Regular Evaluation:** Schedule regular time for self-reflection and evaluation. Analyze your progress, identify areas for improvement, and assess the effectiveness of your current strategies.

- **Embrace Data and Feedback:** Don't operate in a vacuum. Seek feedback from mentors, colleagues, or clients. Utilize data and analytics to track your progress and identify areas needing refinement.

- **Stay Informed:** Keep yourself updated on industry trends and emerging technologies. Continuous learning allows you to identify new strategies and adapt your approach to stay relevant.

- **Experiment and Test:** Don't be afraid to experiment with new approaches. Test different strategies, measure the results, and refine your tactics based on what works best.

- **Embrace Flexibility:** The best strategy is one that adapts to change. Be flexible and willing to adjust your approach as circumstances or your understanding of the situation evolves.

Building a Culture of Continuous Improvement:

Here are some tips to **integrate continuous improvement** into your daily routine:

- **Set SMART Goals:** Clearly define Specific, Measurable, Achievable, Relevant, and Time-bound (SMART) goals. These goals provide a roadmap for your progress and serve as milestones for evaluation.

- **Celebrate Milestones:** Acknowledge and celebrate your achievements, big and small. This reinforces positive behavior and keeps you motivated on your journey.

- **Develop a Growth Mindset:** Believe in your ability to learn and grow. View challenges as opportunities to develop new skills and become a better version of yourself.

- **Seek Continuous Learning:** Never stop learning. Read books, attend workshops, and take courses to expand your knowledge and refine your skillset.

- **Share Your Learnings:** Become a knowledge sharer. Discuss your learnings and experiences with colleagues or mentors. This fosters collaboration and collective improvement.

Remember, continuous improvement is a lifelong journey. Embrace the process, celebrate your progress, and **enjoy the thrill of constant learning and development**. By **refining your strategies**, you can transform challenges into stepping stones and **steadily ascend towards excellence** in all aspects of your life.

Additional Info

Tools, Apps, and Resources to Enhance Productivity

Empower Your Workflow: Tools, Apps, and Resources to Enhance Productivity

Feeling overwhelmed by a never-ending to-do list? Struggling to stay focused and maximize your output? Don't worry, you're not alone. In today's fast-paced world, **productivity** is key to achieving your goals. But fret not, a treasure trove of **tools, apps, and resources** exists to **streamline your workflow** and **boost your efficiency**. Here's your comprehensive guide to **enhancing your productivity** in every aspect of your work life.

Taming the Task Monster: Project Management and Task Organization

Project Management Apps:

- **Asana:** A powerful tool for team collaboration and project organization. Create tasks, assign deadlines, track progress, and foster communication within your team.

- **Trello:** Manage projects with a visual Kanban board system. Move tasks through different stages

(To Do, In Progress, Done) for a clear overview of your workflow.

- **Monday.com:** A highly customizable platform that adapts to your specific needs. Manage projects, tasks, communication, and even automate workflows.

To-Do List Apps:

- **Todoist:** A user-friendly app for creating organized to-do lists. Set priorities, recurring tasks, and deadlines to keep yourself on track.

- **TickTick:** Offers a variety of features like habit tracking and pomodoro timers to boost your focus and productivity.

- **Microsoft To Do:** Integrates seamlessly with other Microsoft products for a cohesive workflow.

Sharpening Your Focus: Time Management and Attention Optimization

Time Management Apps:

- **RescueTime:** Tracks how you spend your time, providing insights into your productivity patterns. Identify time-wasters and adjust your habits accordingly.

- **Focus Keeper:** Utilizes the Pomodoro Technique to promote focused work sessions with short breaks.

- **Forest:** Gamifies productivity by letting you plant a virtual tree. Stay focused, or your tree dies! (Don't worry, it's virtual!)

Focus and Attention Tools:

- **Freedom:** Blocks distracting websites and apps, allowing you to maintain focus on the task at hand.

- **FreedomWriter:** A distraction-free writing environment with a minimalist interface that minimizes distractions.

- **Noisli:** Offers ambient soundscapes to help you tune out distractions and improve focus.

Boosting Your Well-being: Prioritizing Self-Care for Long-Term Success

Mindfulness and Meditation Apps:

- **Headspace:** Guided meditations and mindfulness exercises to reduce stress and improve focus.

- **Calm:** Soothing music, sleep stories, and meditation sessions to promote relaxation and well-being.

- **Insight Timer:** A free app with a vast library of meditations led by experienced teachers.

Habit Tracking Apps:

- **Habitica:** Gamifies habit building by turning your goals into quests and rewards.

- **Streaks:** A simple and elegant app for tracking daily habits and building consistency.

- **Forest:** (Yes, it does double duty!) Track your progress in building healthy habits alongside planting virtual trees.

Here are some additional tips:

- **Don't overload yourself.** Start by integrating a few tools at a time.

- **Focus on quality over quantity.** Prioritize tasks that deliver the most significant results.

- **Schedule regular breaks.** Stepping away from work helps you recharge and maintain focus.

- **Personalize your approach. Craft a system** that aligns with your work style and preferences.

- **Track your progress.** Monitor your productivity and adjust your strategies as needed.

Remember, the key is to find the tools and resources that work best for you. Experiment with different apps and techniques to **discover what optimizes your workflow** and **boosts your productivity.**

Creating a Personalized Productivity System that Works for You

Crafting Your Productivity Powerhouse: A Personalized System for Peak Performance

Feeling overwhelmed by a never-ending to-do list? Struggling to stay focused and achieve your goals? You're not alone. In today's digital age, distractions abound, and maximizing productivity requires a **strategic approach**. The good news is, there's no one-size-fits-all solution. **The key to success lies in creating a personalized productivity system** that caters to your unique work style and preferences.

This guide equips you with a framework to **build a system** that **boosts your efficiency, enhances your focus**, and **empowers you to achieve your goals**.

The Pillars of a Personalized Productivity System:

An effective system rests on four key pillars:

- **Self-Awareness and Goal Setting:** Understanding your strengths, weaknesses, and natural rhythms is crucial. Define clear goals that motivate you and provide direction for your system.

- **Task Management and Prioritization:** Develop strategies to organize your tasks, prioritize effectively, and manage your workload.

- **Focus and Attention Management:** Learn techniques to minimize distractions, maintain focus, and optimize your workflow for deep work.

- **Well-being and Energy Management:** Prioritize your physical and mental well-being to ensure you have the energy and resilience needed for sustained productivity.

Building Your Personalized System: Step-by-Step Guide

Here's how to personalize these pillars and craft a system that works for you:

1. Self-Awareness and Goal Setting:

- **Identify Your Work Style:** Are you an early bird or a night owl? Do you thrive in a quiet workspace or with background noise? Understanding your preferences helps you structure your workday accordingly.

- **Discover Your Strengths and Weaknesses:** What tasks do you excel at? Where do you struggle? Play to your strengths and delegate or outsource weaknesses.

- **Define Your Productivity Goals:** What do you want to achieve? Set SMART goals (Specific, Measurable, Achievable, Relevant, and

Time-bound) to provide direction and track progress.

- **Align Goals with Values:** Ensure your goals reflect your personal values and what's important to you. This fosters intrinsic motivation and a sense of purpose.

2. Task Management and Prioritization:

- **Explore Task Management Techniques:** Experiment with methods like the Eisenhower Matrix, time blocking, or the Pomodoro Technique to find what works best for you.

- **Utilize Tools and Apps:** Leverage project management apps, to-do lists, and time tracking tools to stay organized and manage your workload effectively.

- **Prioritize Ruthlessly:** Not all tasks are created equal. Learn to prioritize ruthlessly, focusing on high-impact activities that drive your goals forward.

- **Schedule Breaks and Buffer Time:** Factor in regular breaks and buffer time between tasks to avoid burnout and allow for unexpected disruptions.

3. Focus and Attention Management:

- **Minimize Distractions:** Silence notifications, turn off social media, and find a quiet workspace to minimize interruptions. Consider tools that block distracting websites or apps.

- **Practice Mindfulness:** Meditation and mindfulness exercises can improve your ability to focus and stay present in the moment.

- **Batch Similar Tasks:** Group similar tasks together to improve focus and minimize context switching.

- **Embrace Technology:** Utilize noise-cancelling headphones, website blockers, or focus apps to create a distraction-free environment.

4. Well-being and Energy Management:

- **Prioritize Sleep:** Getting enough quality sleep is crucial for cognitive function, focus, and overall well-being.

- **Maintain a Healthy Diet:** Eating nutritious meals provides you with sustained energy throughout the day.

- **Exercise Regularly:** Physical activity improves blood flow to the brain, boosting concentration and focus.

- **Manage Stress:** Practice stress management techniques like deep breathing exercises or meditation to maintain a positive and focused mindset.

- **Schedule Breaks for Self-Care:** Take breaks for activities you enjoy to prevent burnout and maintain motivation. Consider a short walk, mindful stretching, or listening to calming music.

Personalization is Key:

- **Experiment and Find Your Flow:** Don't be afraid to experiment with different techniques and tools. Discover what works best for you and your unique work style.

- **Embrace Flexibility:** Your needs and preferences may change over time. Be prepared to adapt your system as necessary.

- **Track Your Progress:** Monitor your productivity and adjust your strategies based on your data and insights.

- **Celebrate Wins:** Acknowledge your achievements, no matter how small. This reinforces positive behavior and keeps you motivated.

Building a personalized productivity system is an ongoing process. Don't get discouraged if you don't get it perfect right away. The key is to **find a system that works for you**, **be consistent in your efforts**, and **celebrate your progress** along the way. Remember, **increased productivity** is a journey, not a destination. Enjoy the ride!

Additional Strategies for Specific Industries or Work Styles

Beyond the Basics: Tailoring Your Productivity System for Specific Industries and Work Styles

While the core principles of a **personalized productivity system** remain constant, **optimizing your workflow** for your specific industry or work style requires **additional strategies**. This guide explores **industry-specific tips** and **work style considerations** to **further enhance your productivity**.

Industry-Specific Strategies:

Creative Fields (Design, Writing, Marketing):

- **Embrace Scheduling with Flexibility:** Schedule dedicated "creative sprints" for focused work, but allow for unstructured brainstorming sessions as well.

- **Curate Inspiration Boards:** Create digital or physical boards to gather inspiration, references, and ideas to keep your creative juices flowing.

- **Utilize Timeboxing for Client Communication:** Allocate specific time slots for checking emails and responding to client inquiries to minimize distractions during creative work.

Information Work (Data Analysis, Research, Law):

- **Master Information Management:** Utilize reference management tools, note-taking apps, and project management software to organize and access information efficiently.

- **Develop Effective Research Strategies:** Learn advanced search techniques and leverage online databases to streamline research processes.

- **Schedule Deep Work Sessions:** Block out uninterrupted time for focused analysis, writing, or reading to maximize concentration.

Project Management and Client Services:

- **Focus on Communication and Collaboration:** Utilize communication tools to keep clients informed, manage expectations, and ensure smooth project flow.

- **Prioritize Task Delegation:** Identify tasks that can be delegated to team members or outsourced to free up your time for higher-level strategic work.

- **Embrace Project Management Methodologies:** Learn and implement project management methodologies like Agile or Waterfall to ensure efficient project delivery.

Sales and Business Development:

- **Prospect Research and CRM Utilization:** Utilize customer relationship management (CRM) tools to organize prospect information and track sales pipelines effectively.

- **Develop a Structured Outreach Process:** Create a system for identifying leads, crafting targeted outreach messages, and scheduling follow-ups.

- **Time Blocking for Sales Calls and Meetings:** Dedicate specific blocks of time for prospecting calls, client meetings, and presentations to maintain focus and momentum.

Work Style Considerations:

- **Early Birds:** Schedule your most demanding tasks for the morning hours when your energy levels are at their peak. Utilize afternoons for meetings or tasks requiring less focus.

- **Night Owls:** Embrace a later workday schedule. Schedule focused work sessions in the evening when there are fewer distractions. Utilize mornings for catching up on emails or administrative tasks.

- **Visual Learners:** Utilize mind maps, flowcharts, and visual aids to organize information and improve task comprehension.

- **Auditory Learners:** Listen to podcasts, audiobooks, or instructional videos while commuting or during breaks to learn and absorb information effectively.

- **Kinesthetic Learners:** Incorporate movement into your workday. Take short walks, stretch breaks, or utilize a standing desk to improve focus and information retention.

Additional Tips:

- **Network with Others in Your Industry:** Connect with colleagues or online communities to share productivity tips and best practices specific to your field.

- **Invest in Professional Development:** Attend workshops, conferences, or take online courses to learn industry-specific productivity strategies and tools.

- **Seek Mentorship:** Find a mentor in your industry who can offer guidance and support in developing your productivity system.

- **Use Dictation Software:** Utilize dictation software to capture ideas and notes without having to type.

- **Record Meetings and Important Discussions:** Record important meetings and discussions to review information later and ensure you haven't missed anything crucial.

Remember, the key is to experiment and find what works best for you. Combine these industry-specific strategies and work style considerations with the core principles of a personalized productivity system to craft a powerful system that optimizes your workflow and propels you towards peak performance.

www.ingramcontent.com/pod-product-compliance
Lightning Source LLC
Chambersburg PA
CBHW071449220526
45472CB00003B/728